Access Is Capture

Access Is Capture

HOW EDTECH REPRODUCES
RACIAL INEQUALITY

Roderic N. Crooks

 UNIVERSITY OF CALIFORNIA PRESS

University of California Press
Oakland, California

Library of Congress Cataloging-in-Publication Data

Names: Crooks, Roderic N., 1973- author.
Title: Access is capture : how edtech reproduces racial inequality / Roderic N.
   Crooks.
Description: Oakland, California : University of California Press, [2024] |
   Includes bibliographical references and index.
Identifiers: LCCN 2024005820 (print) | LCCN 2024005821 (ebook) |
   ISBN 9780520393271 (cloth) | ISBN 9780520393288 (paperback) |
   ISBN 9780520393295 (epub)
Subjects: LCSH: Educational technology—Economic aspects—California—
   Los Angeles. | Segregation in education—Economic aspects—California—
   Los Angeles. | Segregation—California—Los Angeles. | Equality—
   California—Los Angeles.
Classification: LCC LB1028.3 .C7635 2024 (print) | LCC LB1028.3 (ebook) |
   DDC 371.3309794/94—dc371.33 23/eng/20240307
LC record available at https://lccn.loc.gov/2024005820
LC ebook record available at https://lccn.loc.gov/2024005821

Manufactured in the United States of America

33 32 31 30 29 28 27 26 25 24
10 9 8 7 6 5 4 3 2 1

For RODDIE "POPPI" CROOKS (1939–2021),
who taught me the hustle;
and for LEONA McCAFFERY, who taught me the Hustle.

Contents

Acknowledgments

This work, started over a decade ago, has been helped along by many people. I am especially grateful to every teacher, student, security guard, porter, secretary, parent, admin, counselor, librarian, data scientist, analyst, and community organizer who let me look over their shoulder while they worked. Most of the people I talked to in the course of writing this book were also people of color, many of them with roots in the same working-class community that my family comes from, or places very much like it. I have always understood the professional courtesy so reliably extended to me over the years as a form of community care. I hope this book honors that spirit of solidarity, the complexity, beauty, and multifariousness of shared struggle in a relentlessly unequal world.

Portions of the research included in this book were supported by National Science Foundation Award # 2047255 ("Community Organizing for Datafied Worlds") and Award # 1901367 ("Understanding Public Uses of Data and Dashboards"), for which I am tremendously grateful. My writing has also been supported by the Social Science Research Council: thanks to Michael Miller and Catalina Vallejo.

I learned from many deeply accomplished, world-class scholars as a graduate student at UCLA's Graduate School of Education and Information Studies, including Christopher Kelty, Leah Lievrouw, Jean-François Blanchette, and Safiya Noble. I also studied alongside a very talented crew of grad students across Southern California, people who are still at the center of my intellectual and professional life, including my comrades Morgan Currie, Patricia Garcia, Marika Cifor, Seth Erickson, Salvador Zárate, Joan Donovan, Aure Shrock, Dalena Hunter, Kelly Besser, and Angel Diaz. Laurie Russman and the researchers at the Civil Rights Project at UCLA showed me what it takes to make high-quality research in the public interest and to stay at it year after year in the face of threats and harassment.

I am also grateful to the University of California's President's Postdoctoral Fellowship Program: this is a community I always come back to for inspiration, fellowship, and rejuvenation. Immense gratitude to Mark A. Lawson, Kimberly Adkinson, Portia Groce, and Earnestine Harrison for their careful stewardship of our community.

I started an academic career somewhat later in life, without a very detailed understanding of what research in information science might be. Encountering Geoffrey C. Bowker and Susan Leigh Star's book *Sorting Things Out: Classification and Its Consequences* for the first time completely rearranged my mind and gave my scholarly life a direction: in witty and beautiful prose, the book spoke to the very material stakes of racial categories, the gendered dimension of technical labor, and the power of taken-for-granted categories. I had no idea that such books existed or that Geof and his partner Judith Gregory would eventually become wonderful friends, mentors, and intellectual traveling companions.

At UC Irvine, I am so grateful for the friendship and support of the Black Faculty and Staff Association, the Office of Access and Inclusion, and The Black Professoriate of UCI. Our campus community is held down in every capacity by Kevin and Tonya Bradford. For many years, Sharnnia Artis and Doug M. Haynes tended to junior faculty quite lovingly.

At the Bren School of Information and Computer Sciences' Department of Informatics, I've enjoyed the generous mentorship of Paul Dourish, Mimi Ito, Gillian Hayes, Melissa Mazmanian, Anne-Marie Piper, and Kylie Peppler. Rebecca Black and Bill Tomlinson also helped junior faculty keep their heads above water during the first years on the job. Thanks also to the many staff members who have moved the frequently baffling bureaucratic machine that is the university on my behalf, including Ben Rodriguez and Marissa Raymundo. I survived the vicissitudes of junior faculty life with another supportive cohort: Matthew Bietz, Stacy Branham, Tess Tanenbaum, Daniel Epstein, Aaron Trammell, Josh Garcia, Iftekhar Ahmed, and Elena Agapie. It was a great comfort to go through so many professional, personal, and familial transitions with this cadre.

My most frequent academic collaborators over the past half decade have been the talented children of the House of Evocation. Lucy Pei taught me how to write with students and how to win awards. Benedict Salazar Olgado got me together regularly, all while creating tender and beautiful scholarship that meditates on the relationship between databases and human rights. Dr. Uriel Serrano has modeled a kind of community engagement that all of us admire. I am deeply proud of the work current and past members of the Evoke Lab are doing and the concern they show for the communities where they work. The various iterations of the Datafication and Community Activism Workshop have been life-giving.

Grateful also to colleagues Meme Styles, Stephen Molldrem, Alondra Nelson, Lilly Irani, Carl DiSalvo, Tiffany Willoughby-Herard, Jeanne Scheper, Jean Hardy, Tom Boellstorff, Tayloria Adams, Bill Maurer, Tawanna Dillahunt, Britt Paris, Irene Pasquetto, Jennifer Pierre, Daniel Greene, Sheena Erete, Shannon Mattern, Michelle Caswell, Anne Gilliland, Joseph Hankins, Hanna Garth, Greg Leazer, Lilly Nguyen, Ricardo Punzalan, Amelia Acker, Christo Sims, Morgan Ames, Kathy Carbone, Tonia Sutherland, Sarah T. Roberts, Danielle Salomon, Catherine D'Ignazio, Kyle Jones, Amy Vanscoy, Torin Monahan, Christien Tompkins, Dustin O'Hara, and Stacy Wood. Thanks to the University of California Press, to Michelle Lipinski and to the careful, generous reviewers of this text.

To paraphrase the great Patti Labelle, with friends like Jessica Forsyth, Hector Bolanos, and Michael Cherry-Barnes, I'll never go broke.

Thank you to my sisters and brother, who have always been terrific company in good and bad times: Latonya Sankey Johnson (1962–2003), Thursday Peyton, and Derric Crooks. Sending my appreciation also to Hope Jackson Forsythe and to all the uncles, aunties, cousins, nieces, nephews, and niblings who have treated me like a celebrity whenever I came through. Ma and Pa: thank you for being present in our lives. To the loved ones and family members who have joined the ancestors: we remember you and keep you in our hearts. To the family members and loved ones who are locked up still: we remember you and await your safe return.

Finally, deepest gratitude to my husband, Brian Schetzsle, for giving my existence the form and coherence I always longed for, and to our kids, Aidan and Anthony, who have helped me live more thoroughly.

01 Access as Racial Progress

Racial Progress without Race

It is 2014, at a press conference. A researcher's survey results show that Black, brown, rural, and poor households purchase broadband internet connections at lower rates than do other kinds of households. This is bad. He summarizes more surveys revealing that Black people's smartphone ownership rates are highest. This is also bad. There's something different about broadband, the researcher declares, something that cannot be replaced by a mere smartphone's internet service. Over the course of his talk, he explains that broadband is better for homework, for learning to program, for becoming a maker as opposed to a passive consumer of content. The "smartphone-dependent," those who primarily use phones to connect to the internet, are missing out. It's not the device that makes the difference; it's the broadband internet connection. "It's almost like magic," he says. The audience can be heard to applaud vigorously. The researcher smiles reassuringly into the camera, letting the audience know that he has figured out what needs to be done. Something about his message and delivery conveys trust and bonhomie. The magic he is talking about is not shown, but the speaker's honesty convinces the viewer that it must be real. No one else is in the shot—certainly no Black, brown, rural, or poor people, who are also real, but stubbornly committed to buying the wrong, non-magical kind of internet.

It is 2018, in the studied placelessness of a TED studio. A former federal communications commissioner, internet-famous for her bold stance in defense of net neutrality during the Trump administration, delivers an impassioned call for a Digital Civil Rights Bill. She stands in front of a screen emblazoned with the words "Broadband Internet Access / The Greatest Equalizer of Our Time." In contrast to the laconic, minimalist aesthetic of the standard techtalk, her words brim with energy and emotion. She makes you want to nod your head in appreciation:

> For me, and this is a bold statement, the internet is the most enabling, most empowering, most open platform of our times because it meets us where we are, it does not pass judgment, it embraces you and transports you to a place, to a time, to opportunities that man, geography, and other types of limitations would never do.

Offscreen, far away from the podium and the audience, her speech conjures tragic, unknowable specters, cut off needlessly from the necessities of contemporary American life. How or why these victims have become abject is decidedly beside the point because the speaker has preempted any consideration of their predicament with a solution: access to the internet. Her words stir emotion, but they name no culprit. At the end of her talk, the speaker reminds her audience that they have the power to make the future brighter.

She has taken them to church, lifted them up by reminding them of their place in illuminating a grand design.

It is 2023, on the Davos stage, which looks like the set of any morning talk show. A celebrity musician cum entrepreneur speaks of "bridging digital divides" via investment in AI.[1] He is seated across a small table from the interviewer, the two of them placed in the cozy attitude of a press tour, as if the musician had just stopped in for coffee and was then cajoled into promoting a film appearance or a new album. The business reporter interviewing the musician encourages him to extol his own philanthropic successes, setting him up with leading questions that mingle his personal biography, his investments, and his musings on technology. He shouts-out Boyle Heights by name as he recounts boyhood in "inner-city" Los Angeles: with audible frustration, the musician tells of the school-to-prison pipeline, high crime, lack of investment in youth. For each grim and obvious characterization of life in inner-city Los Angeles, his own philanthropic success grows more dramatic, starker. It's got something to do with computers. In a tone that is decidedly matter-of-fact, he says that access to technology is the needed alternative to deleterious conditions in the place where he grew up: "Connectivity should be a human right like drinking water, on tap. It's there. Connectivity should be the same." He speaks of his "recipe" for solving the problems he has cited in talking points he repeats with a mix of boredom and pique, "Technology can help solve the problems we have been struggling with." He seems fed up that he has to keep repeating what is so apparent. The reporter effusively and giddily returns to the success of the musician again and again, inviting him to tout his charity work and his investment strategy to an audience that is hungry for such instruction. He ends with a hush-hush sketch of his next big investment: he has a deal for AI in Africa, but he can't talk about it yet.

At the core of the each of these vignettes, each derived from a public presentation by a technology expert, is a story about access. In these stories, access attaches to a specific technology (broadband service, the internet itself, artificial intelligence) and will be achieved by specific means (philanthropy, a change in regulation, private investment), but the benefits that will accumulate need not be enumerated. These benefits are as real as technology (you can touch them), as undeniable as science (you can believe in them), as inevitable as the future (they are almost here). The subject of the access story is the beneficent technologist who bestows his gifts in order to address the ongoing problems of race, geography, and gender. He is differentiated from other subjects—from "man, geography, and other types of limitations"—because he has made himself unlimited through devotion to technology and rightly derived his power from such industry. That he shares such power willingly marks him as enlightened and enlightening, as capable of making the future brighter.

This book starts and ends with this persistent and appealing trope: the story that pervasive racial inequalities can be addressed through access to some form of computing. In every version of this story, whatever kind of computing technology has been proffered embodies a limitless, futuristic, and benevolent force in a world riven by crusty analog hierarchies. If the disruptions they make are yoked to the right values, it is presumed, a "more human and fair" world will result (Barlow, 1996). The appeal of this access story turns equally on an ideological belief in the power of digital technologies to determine the shape of the future world, and a deep ethical conviction that the benefits of technology to society should be shared in the present, especially with those who have previously been shortchanged by racism, poverty, or precarity. This belief requires an absolute separability and distinction between racism, poverty, precarity, and computing, a commitment that technology is somehow highly active in giving the future world shape, but completely outside the dynamics of present inequalities. While this story about access is tired and may not be as plausible as it once seemed, it still has force. The desire for access motivates investments in public infrastructure; it gives professionals a sense of purpose; it animates massive fundraising efforts and bolsters laws, statutes, and policy.

In the United States, access to technology as an engine of social, political, economic, and racial equality appears against the backdrop of a number of endemic, ubiquitous failures: the failure of Black and brown people to use the proper kinds of computers in appropriate and productive ways; the failure of working-class people to continually cultivate marketable skills; the failure of public schools to confer middle-class status on their racially segregated student bodies. These failures, each a deeply moral indictment, haunt empirical social science and constrain the public imagination. The failures that access to technology is supposed to fix are as varied and changeable as the uneven social terrain produced by racial inequality in the United States and its attendant economic, social, political, and cultural consequences. To fixate on access is a way to take race and other socially consequential forms of difference out of the frame, and to implicitly explain away inequality among people by looking at the distribution of things: computers, routers, cables, software packages, tutorial videos. As many scholars have noted, technology has not only failed to address the structural conditions that reproduce racial inequality; it has, in fact, exacerbated them. Critical scholarship frequently presents this stubborn reality as a case of false consciousness among influential figures in the philanthropic, academic, policy, and tech sectors, as if a few high-minded but credulous figures had seen their innocent technological ambitions deformed by the intrusion of the social world.

In journalism and tech-focused scholarship, these benevolent intentions absolve technologists, academics, policy makers and others from the actual consequences of their relentless efforts to spread, configure, and maintain access on behalf of others. Less remarked upon is how constant investments in various forms of access produce real profits for a variety of actors, although almost never for those whose abjection initially inspired these professional saviors in the first place. Policy and research on access to computing remains doggedly uninterested in the specifics of daily life, technology use, computer non-use, and other aspects of vital significance, including costs associated with getting and keeping access. Questions about the actual benefits of access are thus seen as beyond the reach of cost-benefits analysis and even evidence altogether; who truly benefits from access is no longer an empirical question.

Access has many variations and many adherents, but my interest here is primarily in what happens after this familiar access story is told and enacted: I am thinking about what happens in the aftermath of access. I am less interested in the self-important delusions of tech sector workers or the altruistic gibberish of Silicon Valley philanthropists; instead, I want to think with and about the everyday experiences of people who live, study, and work with modes of access that have been foisted on them for one reason or another. I am thinking not of professional trendsetters or evangelists who craft better futures for the rest of us to buy, but of the teachers, students, parents, and organizers who have to get on with the business of living in communities hollowed out by public disinvestment, gentrification, and over-policing. I am thinking of people who roll their eyes, wait a beat, then get on with what they were trying to say; of people who improvise, work around, cheat, hack, half-ass, and ignore with great creativity and style. I am thinking of people who may or may not put stock in the vision of a liberatory technological future, but who will nonetheless find ways to pursue their own programs and solve their own problems with whatever materials are at hand.

In this book, I put two sociological concepts into play to look differently at access to technology: *racial formation* and *datafication*. These important concepts are widespread in many fields of research but have not been applied together meaningfully. In what follows, I center sociological concepts and racial analysis in the study of technology. Race is central to how technology operates and what it does in the world (or perhaps more accurately, what technology does to whom), despite the obfuscating tendency of racial dynamics with respect to technology use to be washed away with cynical "color-blind" dogma (Daniels, 2015). Datafication is a useful and capacious theory that reveals powerful cultural frames of reference able to influence policy and daily life in pervasive ways. It helps to explain how technological change happens, and how its benefits accrue toward powerful interests. Putting these ideas together, I use racial formation, particularly the concept of the *racial project*, to evaluate datafication, to see how it both trades on and extends ideas about immutable racial difference and white superiority through the creation, aggregation, and circulation of data, much of it captured by technologies distributed in the name of access.

Access as Racial Project

In the years immediately following the commercial expansion of the internet, Nelson et al. (2001) placed the study of race at the center of the study of digital technologies. The authors connected Henri Lefebrve's work on everyday life to a variety of issues in contemporary digital media, focusing on the "extra-technical" meaning of technological artifacts and the affective dimensions of technologies that give them "productive force" (p. 4). This productive force functioned over and was refracted through the fundamentally uneven and unequal terrain of the social world, by the complexities of lived experiences of racial difference. The authors argued that digital technologies, even when deployed to address "historical exclusions," blurred the lines between democratic virtue and profit (p. 5).

Still, this early and now seemingly prescient work represents in the main something of a road-not-taken by technology-focused, social scientific research—including social informatics, science and technology studies, and human-computer-interaction. As I have written elsewhere (Crooks, 2022), technology-focused scholarship frequently ignores race. While the particulars of technology applied to public life have clear implications for the management of racialized subjects by state and capital, the imbrication of race and digital technology has frequently been overlooked or marginalized in technology-focused scholarship, even as theories and terms developed in scholarship on race have enjoyed greater scholarly and popular circulation (e.g., critical race theory, intersectionality). Research in new media studies and communication (authored mostly by Black women scholars and other scholars of color) has insisted for many years now that the study of digital technologies and media requires attention to race (Nakamura & Chow-White, 2012; Noble & Tynes, 2015). For example, Coleman (2009) directly links race and technology, arguing for a conceptual shift in how to define race, a proposition that "moves race away from the biological and genetic systems that have historically dominated its definition toward questions of technological agency" (p. 177). Coleman's approach to making race synonymous with technology is also a tactic repeated by Benjamin (2019) (albeit with very different commitments), who argues that race itself is a technology and that the study of technology is always already racial: Benjamin fruitfully combines approaches from science studies and critical race theory. In studies shaped by biomedical research and genomics, Bliss (2013) and Nelson (2016) address the significance of commercial genetic ancestry testing. In very different contexts, they examine the complexity and durability of race not only in its medical, informational, and genetic dimensions, but also in its affective, economic, and cultural aspects. McMillan Cottom (2020) points to the overriding incoherence of scholarship on the sociology of the internet and proposes a conceptual apparatus for contemporary sociological research at the intersection of platform studies and racial capitalism.[2] There certainly exist rich, beautiful writings that explore connections between race and technology in creative, careful, and rigorous ways. However, as Safiya Noble has argued, a glib approach to the incorporation of Black and Black feminist intellectual approaches has prevented much tech-focused research from meaningfully examining "the global distributions of resources that disproportionately and negatively impact Black life, and the lives of those in the Global South, in the material creation, use, and disposal of digital technology" (Noble, 2016). Regrettably, academic research on technology has frequently been unable to refute the prevailing dogma that the design, use, and societal implications of technology have nothing to do with race, especially in terms of tech policy and undergraduate education.[3]

Race is, of course, complex, and there is no single, unitary social scientific definition of what it is. But in terms of research, there are fairly established (although frequently conflictual) accounts of how to study what race does in the world. While *race* is a term of prescientific origins that contemporary scholars of all kinds have used as a lens or object of study, *racialization* is a more recent social scientific term frequently attributed to the sociological theory of racial formation (Martinez HoSang & LaBennett, 2020). Building from historical explorations of political struggle, popular culture, and public policy in the United States, Omi and Winant (2016) have notably defined *racial formation* as "the sociohistorical process by which racial categories are created, inhabited, transformed, and destroyed" (p. 379). From this perspective, race is socially constructed (as opposed to naturally occurring) and politically contested (as opposed to biologically deterministic). This theory rebuts any potential biological warrant for racial categories, and instead presents such categorizations as historically produced for the benefit of some at the expense of others. Hegemonic racial formations precede and shape individual subjectivity and, like all systems of classification, confer powerful advantages upon their beneficiary classes (Bowker & Star, 1999). Racial categories then do not originate from any stable set of naturally occurring, in-group characteristics. Rather, racial classifications "are intimately linked to politics and power that rely on coercion (i.e., violence, threats, and pressure) and consent for their existence" (Keaton, 2018).

Of critical significance to this book's analysis of the highly skilled work of teachers, data professionals, and community organizers, racialization occurs simultaneously across multiple scales and modalities, wherever and whenever "human bodies and social structures are represented and organized" (Omi & Winant, 2016, p. 380). "Racialization" describes the dynamic action of racial formations and how they govern the experiences of individuals, groups, the state, and other collectivities. The term emphasizes an active process, the way categories precede the collections of qualities they claim merely to describe. Racial formation theory gives us the concept of the *racial project*:

> *A racial project is simultaneously an interpretation, representation, or explanation of racial dynamics, and an effort to reorganize and redistribute resources along particular racial lines.* Racial projects connect what race means in a particular discursive practice and the ways in which both social structures and everyday experiences are racially organized, based upon that meaning. (p. 380, italics in original)

Racial projects—as well as the implicated racial categories they animate and enforce—are sites of struggle where competing group interests, systems of language, and modes of representation collide. The state is a prime site of racial projects, where law, science, technology, citizenship, media, and protest meet in complex conflicts with lasting social consequences for the allocation of vital resources (Ferguson, 2020). In this book I argue that data in all its forms, especially digital data tied up with the real and imagined capacities of computers, contributes powerfully to racial projects, to representations of people and the perceived regularity of their characteristics according to racist hierarchies and to the resultant distribution of needed resources and services.

An emphasis on the state is important to my work here for a few reasons. First, for over a decade now, I have been studying technology as it is incorporated in public education. Public education is certainly worth studying in its own right, but as many other critical scholars have noted, public education is both the site of extreme racial inequality and a state-sponsored undertaking of vast cultural importance. Education is also, not coincidentally, a site of relentless technological experimentalism. The contemporary education technology ("edtech") sector, a menagerie of thousands of apps, platforms, tools, websites, and devices used in the delivery of education, is projected to reach a value of nearly $400 billion by 2026 (Korhonen, 2024). In the following chapters, I will look at the forms that some of these experiments with technology in public education have taken to show how educational technology is wrapped up with extreme racial and economic inequality. Both public education and the tech sector are nurtured, funded, and actively shaped by the state: they are racial projects.

Second, technology research, influenced and practiced as it is by many commercial concerns, has frequently focused on atomized users as a unit of analysis. The user is an important type, but in the contexts that I am interested in here, the user fits rather uneasily with other preestablished roles. When trying to understand the use of an app, platform, or device, thinking of a person as a user does not necessarily arouse suspicion. But the insertion of an app, platform, or device into some vital public function where its use becomes a requirement opens up a space for commercial interests in the extraction of rents and profits, where we otherwise might not have allowed such middle-manning. In short, we do not always aspire to be users of democratic institutions; sometimes we wish to be participants, citizens, subjects, teachers, students, parents, children, and so on (Day, 2011). I am also interested in better understanding how collectivities engage with technology. Use of technology entails relations of power and authority, not just for individual persons, but for communities, residents, neighborhoods, families, diasporas, and so on.

Third, as my comrade Daniel Greene has asserted persuasively in *The Promise of Access: Technology, Inequality, and the Political Economy of Hope* (2021), the promotion of greater access to technology in the United States is a guiding logic of federal policy on education, communication, and intellectual property. His book looks at tech solutionism and digital divide narratives, specifically focusing on programs that depend on "the access doctrine"—the idea that the proper technological tools can fix poverty. Greene's sharp ethnographer's eye visits several organizations, including a technology startup, a public library, and a charter school in Washington, D.C. He uses the term *bootstrapping* to describe how public organizations are forced to reconfigure themselves in the image of the tech sector (an apt description of the process at play in the next three chapters). Greene's book situates the persistent technological solutionism of access-based approaches within a political economy analysis of the professional-managerial class, an analysis that encourages librarians and other information professionals to find common cause with users and patrons of underfunded public institutions, and teachers whose workplaces have been upended by technological hype and austerity.

The goal of my emphasis on the state and public life is to analyze access to technology in a way that does not present access as an error in need of correction, but as a purposive, seductive, and even desirable way of thinking about racial progress.[4] Racial formation theory helps us zoom out from the preferences of this or that atomized and idealized user to better understand why the prevailing vision of technology as a tool of racial progress has so much allure, even as analysis of race has been relatively rare in technology-focused research and nearly absent in popular discussions of the tech sector and its products. Racial formation theory historicizes the ongoing redefinition of racial categorizations, placing particular emphasis on the current state of racial formation on the post–civil rights era in the United States. In the backlash against the mass movements of the 1960s and cultural and political struggles that ensued, color-blind racism developed as a tactic for entrenched powers to continue to distribute resources according to racial hierarchies, especially via larger processes of state investment and disinvestment. Color-blind racism "rationalizes the status of minorities as the product of market dynamics, naturally occurring phenomena, and their alleged cultural deficiencies" (Bonilla-Silva & Dietrich, 2011, p. 191). Color-blind racism thrives in the tech sector, including higher education in science, technology, engineering, and mathematics, where it "helps sustain an analogous set of beliefs about tech industry leaders' own White racial innocence and blamelessness in a racially unequal society" (Daniels, 2015, p. 1383).

I view American public life as a series of overlapping and interconnected racial projects: in the United States, the public sphere is defined, constituted, and managed according to the specific interests of an elite group that is racialized as white (Ferguson, 2012; Martinez HoSang & LaBennett, 2020; Muñoz, 1999). As opposed to terms like *underrepresented*, *minority*, and *underserved*, this book uses the term *minoritized* to bring attention to the historical specificity of American racial and sexual hierarchy in public life (Ferguson, 2004; Muñoz, 1999). This term emphasizes power relations rather than demography, and draws attention to how conventional rules about appropriate behavior in the public sphere function for the benefit of an unmarked, unraced, and ungendered ideal, while all other forms of socially sanctioned difference mark varying degrees of inferiority. Public life incorporates strictures that apply differently to different kinds of people, effectively creating de facto racial codes about who and what can exist in public (Browne, 2015).

Critically, race is perhaps the primary mode by which people in the United States are ranked, sorted, and dealt with in terms of life chances, but race itself can never occur in isolation because "the major systems of oppression are interlocking" (Combahee River Collective, 1977, p. 271). Every raced person in the United States is also gendered, has a citizenship status, and so on, in a web of prismatic overlappings. Minoritized peoples—those "differentially valued by their ordered relation to capital"—will find their lower status in the hierarchy everywhere articulated in representational, symbolic, cultural, legal, and aesthetic systems that justify the unequal distribution of resources according to a naturalized, white supremacist, patriarchal order (Allen, 2021, p. 6).

Calls for access to technology in schools, libraries, and other youth-serving institutions then co-occur with the persistent, racialized public inequalities that shape minoritized communities in the United States. This is not a coincidence. Part of what makes access to technology so appealing is that it offers a way to address inequality among minoritized peoples without having to identify or name the racism and structural oppressions that shape the life chances of all people. Avoiding these realities with the salve of "magical thinking" of access to technology is not just injurious to some groups of people (Eubanks, 2011); it is also quite beneficial to others.

How Access Happens When It Happens to Us

Like many working-class Black people, I was raised to revere education, to believe that even if I had to work twice as hard as another (presumably white) student to get half as much recognition, I should consider myself lucky to be able to go to school in the first place. The experience (not the memory, but the visceral, embodied, firsthand experience) of Jim Crow was never far from my family: my grandmother, though she spoke of it only reluctantly, was a daughter of Mississippi. She grew up as one of thirteen children of a rural sharecropper and came west as part of the Great Migration. My father himself, though there was no trace of it in his suave and urbane bearing, had been born in Mississippi and come to California as a toddler. None of the family elders told us much about Mississippi, but we all felt the momentum of our collective flight. Later, I learned via social studies classes in mostly white schools about the dogs and the firehoses and the marches. By the time I was born, my family had become multiracial and fully Californian, invested in the idea that my grandmother's great journey had made freedom possible for the younger generation, if only we were industrious enough to pursue it and disciplined enough to remember where we came from. Being a bookish and shy person, I took to schooling as if my life depended on it, because in some ways, it did. It did not take long for my love of books to turn into a love of computers. When I became a doctoral student, my unquestioning commitment to education had become an unquestioned belief in the value of access to technology for working-class students of color like myself. I started fieldwork in a South Los Angeles high school not far from where my father grew up, to learn firsthand *how* access to technology happens. I imagined my research would generate a whole catalog of wonderful and creative uses of digital technology by clever students and teachers, one that might inspire more investment from the state or prove to technologists that people like us were capable of using computers in respectable ways.

What I found in the school I first studied, and in my later research on professionals charged with making sense of the digital data that access to technology brought into circulation, was a great deal of ambivalence. Digital technologies were important to many different groups of people, certainly, but to understand which groups could use technology for their own advantage was more complicated than I had imagined. Moreover, digital technology demanded a great many resources from the people, organizations, and communities where it was deployed. Who received those resources, and who provided them, is also what this book is about.

My own thinking about digital technology and its role in the racial oppression that creates and maintains minoritized communities went through many changes during the years of my research. In 2017, during some of the field work described in later chapters of this book, the Los Angeles chapter of a Black Lives Matter-aligned group announced via Facebook a monthly open meeting at Chuco's Justice Center, a community center dedicated to "youth lost to the streets, prisons, police violence or deportation" (Youth Justice Coalition, 2019). During the previous three months, a number of spontaneous demonstrations, walk-outs, marches, occupations, and other forms of protest flourished all around Los Angeles, many of them staged in working-class and poor Black and Latinx[5] neighborhoods. Youth of color, many of whom felt personally and collectively threatened by the presidential inauguration of Donald Trump that January, were frequent instigators of and participants in these demonstrations. At Chuco's, on the border of

South-Central Los Angeles and Inglewood, hundreds of people, most of them apparently from other neighborhoods, assembled in a show of support for the international Black Lives Matter movement. As the hour of the meeting drew nearer, a crowd full of predominantly white hipsters wrapped around the block, many of them surreptitiously snapping selfies. Others telegraphed scorn for such blatant self-regard. A twentysomething Black woman waiting near me admonished no one in particular (and everyone in general) that she had seen no such crowd the month before and would be shocked to see any such thing the month following, much less the month after. No one seemed sure what kind of behavior the occasion demanded, whether visitors to the center should be boisterous or respectful. Another young woman worked her way down the line from the jammed front door to ask that Black people be given priority to enter the building, and had to repeat this request every three feet or so to be heard. Cops watched the crowd disdainfully from cruisers parked in the middle of the street.

The atmosphere in line was tense and quiet, more funeral than political rally. The size of the crowd seemed to have caught the organizers of the meeting off-guard: they had no real crowd-control measures or public address system in place. I felt frustrated that the meeting was not ready to receive me, that my support had no channel to find expression. I also felt stung by the admonitions of the more experienced meeting-goers about supporting the organization more seriously, beyond tacky photo opportunities. I was unsure whether or not I would be read by the core group of event organizers (all of whom were young Black women) as local, as belonging inside at the meeting, rather than outside with the hipsters. Eventually, the organizers found voice amplification equipment and used it to direct the crowd to nearby Roosevelt Park, where the meeting turned into a spontaneous rally in the outdoor auditorium. The organizers ended up giving the crowd what it wanted, in the form of chants, speeches, and a carnival vibe. I resolved to find some way to reorient my own activist efforts into something more useful and more original than filling my social media feeds with pictures of myself looking righteous. I took a copy of the monthly schedule of meetings on my way back to the car.

A few days later, I attended a drop-in meeting of a prison abolition group, mostly because it took place during the week, when I thought fewer people would be available to show their support, and because I admired the organization's work. Years before I had seen Angela Davis give a talk on abolition in New York City, just blocks away from the prison where she was once held during the events depicted in her autobiography (a book I lovingly read and reread in my youth). Due partly to my family's experience of mass incarceration, I have never *not* been an abolitionist. I was raised seeing and believing that the criminal justice system was an instrument of Black Americans' political and economic oppression. I did not yet describe myself as an abolitionist, but I certainly held the view that police harmed rather than helped people, and that prisons like those that had frequently held my father and other family members were forms of contemporary slavery, links in a heavy chain that bound us to Jim Crow and to Mississippi cotton fields and to the ships and whatever came before. I knew many people who were in or had been to the penitentiary, and nearly all of them were working-class Black people from families like mine who were locked up for illicit forms of economic activity.

The event did not meet my expectations: the host of the drop-in meeting was a very young-looking white girl who explained that she was a UC Berkeley undergraduate home in L.A. while taking time off from her degree. Other than the host, there were only two other volunteers who had joined the drop-in event: a young white man whom I did not hear speak once and a very enthusiastic Latinx kid who lived in the neighborhood and went to community college close by. The purpose of the meeting was to make posters for an upcoming rally in support of a multi-organization action in opposition to the construction of new prisons in California. Mandy, the host, ordered Domino's pizza and asked if I had any questions about the Prison-Industrial Complex. She had provided various poster making materials—cardboard, markers, tempera paint—and suggested several mottos form which to choose: "No More Prisons," "Schools Not Prisons," "Free Them All." I felt over-qualified to be coloring posters, but no other vehicle for my activist energies had been provided. I also felt awkwardly positioned by my ambiguous relationship to the neighborhood the Justice Center serves: I felt a need to be recognized as a local, but also felt that status to be tenuous, suspect even. After a halting start to conversation with Mandy (and a suspicious gaze from the local kid, imagined perhaps), I told her about my doctoral studies at UCLA, and The conversation turned to a topic that was easier for me to get excited about: data.

It turned out that Mandy and the local chapter of the organization she worked with did not have exact information on what prisons were already in existence in California. In The week after the poster session, I set about trying to inform Mandy. Using Wikipedia, Google Maps, and public websites such as the one maintained by the California Department of Corrections and Rehabilitation, I assembled a list of all the prison facilities maintained by the state of California. The spreadsheet included the name of each facility, the number of people it could hold, what kinds of people it housed (e.g., men, women, children), its locality, its latitude and longitude, and so on. I included links to official websites for those facilities that maintained such resources. The first iteration of the project took me roughly ten hours to complete. Looking at the list, however, I noticed that it did not include facilities I knew about from personal experience, including the Twin Towers, a notorious jail run by the Los Angeles County Sheriff's Department. Working from other public sources such as the Sheriff's Department website, I added all the jails I could find, including county-run detention centers. Lastly, I pieced together another set of jails, those run by the Los Angeles Police Department. Again, based on my own personal and familial experience, I knew that these facilities existed, even if no centralized, comprehensive public data source included them alongside other kinds of jails. I knew my list was partial, since I did not include other county and city jails outside Southern California: there had to be dozens or hundreds more jails in the state.

When I emailed Mandy the document, including a note on its limitations, her praise was effusive. "This is AWESOME," she emailed, which is exactly what I wanted to hear. I had contributed needed data work: bloodless, remote, efficient. That such work was possible because I had garnered particular skills through decades of attendance at majority white schools (including the University of California, Los Angeles) satisfied me deeply. More, this was but the beginning: I had worked for years in the tech sector and also recently taken classes in ArcGIS, SQL, and information retrieval. I had a lot more technical tricks in my bag, tricks that might earn me the praise of movement types such as Mandy and contribute to what I understood to be a long, ongoing struggle. This struggle included Angela Davis, my father, all the other family members who had ever been jailed, our family's escape from Mississippi, our devastating loss of the family home to gentrification, the suspicious teenager, and my deep desire to contribute to the freedom and dignity of my community of origin. That this full-circle opportunity came in the form of a spreadsheet gave me hope that the peripatetic and unconventional professional and academic journey I had pursued for two decades had added up to something useful, that I—who had enjoyed a freedom of movement and educational opportunity that my father and his mother had never known—would make good on what I had been given. If working on data meant working on racial justice, then I could easily contribute to the movements and communities that academic life had separated me from. In the long struggle for freedom, Black Americans have always deployed cultural and affective forms that inspired, coordinated, and directed intergenerational struggle, so the development of datalogical forms of resistance seemed to my mind both necessary and inevitable. There are many ways to contribute to shared struggle, some visible and public, others subtle and localized. As previous generations of people had adopted whatever tools were at hand to fight for the freedom of all oppressed people, techies could use the computational tools of our time to carry on the part of the struggle that is both our proud inheritance and our deepest debt.

In time, I came to view this understanding of the continuity of struggle as naive, but at that moment, my work in graduate school, my field work in the schools and school systems of South Los Angeles, and the work of community organizing spoke to each other in a way that let me glimpse something I had long suspected was there but that I could never pin down or explain, a kind of digital data circulation that connected the desire for racial justice with the many kinds of extractions and slippages I was cataloging. This vision amounted to a narrow, provisional space where the genuine attempts of people to make themselves free via intergenerational struggle met the relentlessly ahistorical and laudatory claims of technological change.

"What Can I Do? It's the Future"

Technological change is a multivalent concept: It refers to material transformation of the built world, to progressive, ongoing processes of evolution and, equally, to the sudden jolt of the new. Despite its frequent characterization as a fast-moving visitant that shapes human endeavors—the arrival of "the computer" and its meteoric impacts on the social terrain—technological change is a familiar rhetorical starting point. For decades, many kinds of research have begun with the unquestioned assertion that some technological revolution has suddenly unsettled some other collective undertaking. What if, instead of thinking about the discontinuities and ruptures of some process called technological change, we were instead to make analytical use of the way that technological change has achieved permanence? Although my argument arrives eventually at characterizing contemporary notions of data-intensive computing applied to the education of Black and Latinx children in working-class South Los Angeles, it applies potentially to any domain where people yoke public doings to the charming and seductive capacities of computers, what J. C. R. Licklider (1960) characterized as "men and computers working together in intimate association" (p. 5). From this angle, in addition to being an observation of some trend or set of conditions, technological change is also a normative demand, a command to move around resources, for example. As Andre Brock (2019) has consistently reiterated, computers have many functions, including ideological functions: that's part of what technology is. Because it is seen as inevitable, technological change justifies many programs and interventions. As one of my respondents answered when I asked him why it was a priority to give every student in his school some kind of computer, "My son has an iPad. He's only two years old. I don't even want him to have one, but what can I do? It's the future."

So within this zone called technological change, the change is always happening and inevitable, but also, paradoxically, requires all kinds of investment, installation, maintenance, troubleshooting, upgrading, and care work. Especially as it concerns minoritized communities, the powerful demand for access can rarely be questioned by everyday people or even by experts. But access is never finished, once and for all. Access is merely the first and necessary precondition for whatever comes next. The demand for access enjoins the public to configure a resource field, to buy computing technology and try to install it, at a minimum, hopefully keep it operational or get people to use it, if possible. In the case that the next chapter focuses on, public investment in access to technology merely sets the stage for other kinds of extractions. And, although there are many kinds of extractions at work, this book will focus primarily on data.

Sociological research has captured the way technological change operates in the first decades of the twentieth century with the term *datafication*. In its empirical sense, datafication refers to the representation and mediation of some aspect of social life by digital data, "the phenomenon of quantifying aspects of life that previously did not exist numerically" (Kennedy & Hill, 2016, p. 3). In this sense, the term keeps alive the idea that something new has already begun, the feeling that we are always beginning our stories about technology in medias res. Like the research of previous decades organized around the process of *computerization*, datafication turns on how "computer systems can restructure social relationships by altering the kinds of information readily available" and alter "patterns of access to information" (Kling, 1991, p. 344). But researchers interested in datafication have also pointed out that what is mainly of interest when modes of sociality become mediated by computers and the data they create, capture, and process, are the beliefs and values that impel such remediation in the first place. Datafication, as I use the term in my own research, names a species of technological change and points to a concomitant set of beliefs concerning what data is and what it can do. As it is commonly understood by everyday people as well as many kinds of professional researchers, data has the power to act as proxy for any person, place, or thing. There is a logical and egalitarian metaphysics at work in thinking about digital data this way: everything can be represented by data and therefore, everything can be made subject to the powers of computation. Computation, if correctly executed, creates a predictable and orderly world, one governed by the laws of statistics and the rule of mathematics. Datafication imagines a universe mimetically captured via digital data, a world of latent patterns waiting to be revealed.

But data is not, as datafication might have it, some inert, neutral, mathematical description of the world; it is a significant material force in shaping the world.[6] The current conception of data draws on both the developments of computer science—the ever-growing calculative power of networked computers as promoted in Rand Corporation diagrams and Moore's Law illustrations—and the nineteenth-century growth of modern forms of the bureaucratic state. Muhammad (2010) historicizes the creation and circulation of "racial data," the quantified description of Black abjection in the form of crime, health, marriage, and employment metrics, arguing that such quantitative descriptors give government agencies speciated subjects to govern. Ultimately, racial data is the foundation of both modern sociology and the bureaucratic forms of the contemporary state; it renders suspect the supposed objectivity of data in public decision-making. Data is how the state sees its subjects and itself (Scott, 1998), in a vision that involves a form of willful ignorance, an unwillingness to take in the whole. Data might reveal patterns, but it is also an effective way of keeping selected subjects and objects out of sight, unseen, and unseeable. These distinct genealogies of data—of computer science and of institutional bureaucracy—inflect the contemporary understanding of data as something that should guide public action as well as something that is given by the world itself (Crooks & Currie, 2021). However, despite the cultural associations it has acquired, part of data's great appeal has always been its ability to describe and categorize racial subjects.

In the context of contemporary American datafication, minoritized subjects in general and Black people in particular are simultaneously hyper-exposed as targets of surveillance regimes in which they are unwillingly enrolled, profoundly invisible, dehumanized, and misgendered by sensing systems poised to become central to public life (Browne, 2015; Buolamwini, & Gebru, 2018). From the perspective of racial projects, contemporary, networked, and data-intensive computation makes possible new forms of enclosure and extraction for communities constrained by hierarchies of race, class, gender, sexuality, disability, citizenship, and other overlapping and co-present identity differentials (Noble, 2018; Combahee River Collective, 1977).

Much more could be said of the similarities between computerization research and the recent paradigm of datafication, but for the purposes of this book, it will suffice to say this: despite the frequent emphasis on novelty and newness in scholarship on technology and critical scholarship concerning education, technological change has achieved a remarkably stable rhetorical horizon, one characterized not only by promises of change, improvement, or solutions—but also by failure, error, and defeat. In other words, part of what sets the stage for the evidence-defying assertions of access's value for this or that education technology (especially with respect to students rendered at-risk or underrepresented) is an invocation of failure for some and not others. Failure too relies on a set of background beliefs and norms about performance, accountability, and agency. Access, then, uses these cultural materials: access is that place where the failure of people to do what they ought to meets the generative, intimate, seductive powers of computation. It is also the place where the possibilities of a datafied world order and reorder the stubborn, uncooperative, unglamourous daily routines of teachers, students, workers, and citizens.

Urban Schools as Enclosure

Historically, educators have incorporated different kinds of emerging media and technologies into learning and instruction as they become more affordable and widespread—radio, film, video, CCTV, the internet, laptop computers, mobile devices, apps, and platforms. These technologies embody cultural values about what it means to be an American at a certain place and time. This pattern obtains for pre-electronic technologies as well, which were included in public education at the turn of the twentieth century to educate American students in progressive ideals of cosmopolitanism and awareness of the extent of U.S. empire (Good, 2020). Data-intensive technologies have been controversial when applied to American public education, particularly as they concern spending priorities and student privacy. On the one hand, proponents argue that automated analysis of data can make possible individualized study plans, independent measurement of student learning, and new kinds of pedagogical tools to replace antiquated modes of teaching (Knox et al., 2019; Slade & Prinsloo, 2013). On the other hand, many educators, theorists, and activists question the introduction of new forms of technology into public education out of concern over utility, student privacy, or the commercial nature of digital platforms and software (King et al., 2016; Thompson & Cook, 2013). In important ways, both proponents and critics of data-driven edtech make similar assumptions about the value and self-evidence of educational data, a point I will return to in later chapters.

Nowhere is the appeal of access used to justify public expenditures on edtech more pronounced than in urban schools. In education research, the term *urban schools* refers to those racially segregated, high-poverty schools that serve minoritized communities, primarily Black and Latinx, frequently in city centers once hollowed out by white flight and now the site of intense housing displacement and gentrification (Buras, 2014; Erickson, 2016; Pearman & Swain, 2017). In these public school settings, edtech is frequently touted as a corrective to the social, economic, or technological manifestations of racialized poverty. In recent years, urban schools and school districts have adopted various kinds of hardware and software products to address persistent and worsening conditions of racial segregation and economic precarity. These fixes have included one-to-one computer programs (Ames, 2016); hybrid online/in-person "blended" learning scenarios (Rasheed et al., 2020); after-school programs and informal learning (Garcia & Morrell, 2013); design-based curricula (Sims, 2017), and, most recently, data-intensive computation (Fricchione et al., 2021). These edtech fixes come at a time when the basic principles and ends of U.S. public education have become unsettled, as evidenced by a policy consensus that blames under-resourced schools themselves for failing to produce equity in minoritized communities (Erickson, 2016). Post-pandemic, urban schools, like other public schools, face declining enrollment, hostile political oversight from organized right-wing political interests, and teacher shortages.

During the seven years I was a graduate student at UCLA, I worked for the Civil Rights Project at UCLA, a research unit led by Professors Patricia Gándara and Gary Orfield (and skillfully administered by Laurie Russman, who remained charming and humorous despite frequent death threats related to the work of the center). Researchers at the CRP have produced an extensive volume of high-quality, detailed quantitative research about racial segregation in U.S. K–12 schools, including meticulous reports about each state in the union. The argument CRP researchers have made over the years is simple, consistent, and clear: U.S. schools are more racially segregated than when the Supreme Court ruled de jure segregation to be a violation of the Constitution in 1954. Of K–12 schools in California, Orfield et al. (2019) write,

> White and Latino students are the most segregated groups. White students, on average, attend a school in which 69% of the students are white, while Latino students attend a school where 55% of the students are Latino. Segregation for Black students is rising in all parts of the U.S. Black students, who account for 15% of enrollment

as they did in 1970, are in schools that average 47% Black students. Asian students, on average, attend schools with 24% fellow Asians. Black students attend schools with a combined Black and Latino enrollment averaging 67%, and Latino students attend schools with a combined Black and Latino enrollment averaging 66%. White and Asian students have much lower exposure to combined Black and Latino students, at 22% and 34%, respectively." (p. 4–5)

Urban schools, as intensely racially segregated learning environments, are also frequently sites of "double segregation," where students of lower socioeconomic status are concentrated; this double segregation amounts to a "disproportionate exposure to concentrated poverty," further harming and stigmatizing affected public school students (Orfield et al., 2019, p. 24). Regardless of the quality of education their institutions offer, Black students who attend racially segregated schools are "inordinately" harmed by racial segregation, as well as segregation based on socioeconomic status (Palardy et al., 2015). Students from other minoritized communities are likewise harmed. Such harm is part of the neglected context that access obscures. Access looks promising and even vital when the background against which it appears is generational, racialized precarity.

My focus on access to edtech in urban schools is both professional and personal. It stems from both my interest in the working-class and poor communities where I was born and my scholarly writing about race in public life. Urban schools arise largely as a consequence of racial and economic segregation in housing. They are frequently faulted for failing to produce economic mobility in their student bodies or lauded for tough approaches intended to guide students toward favorable, against-the-odds outcomes. However, this way of thinking about them ignores the way that urban schools themselves support the racial project of U.S. education policy, according to which quality public education is a resource to be distributed along racial lines. Moreover, racial projects are material and discursive—that is, they function to make specific systems appear as the natural consequence of racial difference. The commonsense failure of urban schools structures both popular understandings and policy decisions about education. To speak of public education as a collection of tools, techniques, and programs separate from the racial inequality that produces them situates the minoritized communities served by urban schools as in need of reform or intervention by private enterprise and the tech sector (Au, 2016).

Urban schools are highly disciplined environments where data produced through new edtech supports established regimes of accountability and surveillance, be they analog, digital, or something in -between (Mirón & St. John, 2003; Taylor, 2013). As my mentors at CRP have frequently found, disciplinary measures in urban schools harm Black, Latinx, and/or disabled students, who are "frequently subjected to exclusionary practices, excessive policing, and the denial of an equitable opportunity to learn" (Losen et al., 2022, p. 2). Activists and sympathetic researchers have coined the term *school-to-prison pipeline* to describe this dynamic of urban schools, where emphasis on student behavior and administrative overreaction to perceived safety violations have been found to shunt children (and parents) minoritized by race, class, disability, and/or citizenship out of public education and into the criminal justice system (Meiners, 2011; Raible & Irizarry, 2010). Though reformers and policy experts have argued for changes and adjustments to the highly reactive measures and strict policies that urban schools use to discipline their student bodies, other scholars, activists, and community members have underscored the deep, abiding, and seemingly unbreakable link between schools and prisons.

Writing of such schools in California, my colleague Damian Sojoyner has movingly critiqued the notion of the school-to-prison pipeline in his book *First Strike: Educational Enclosures in Black Los Angeles* (Sojoyner, 2016). As Sojoyner describes it, the school-to-prison pipeline misunderstands the relationship between schools and prisons, as if the two institutions were distinct, or could somehow allow particular kinds of schooling or individual behaviors to steer students into more or less desirable futures. Sojoyner proposes a conceptual shift instead to think of both public education and the prison system as enclosures of Black life, and by extension, life for other minoritized or multiply minoritized communities:

> Enclosure is representative of social mechanisms that construct notions of race, gender, class, and sexuality; and just as important as the imposition of the physical and unseen, enclosure embodies the removal/withdrawal/denial of services and programs that are key to the stability and long-term well-being of communities (p. xiii).

This relationship between schools and prisons is critical for the following chapters and is a fact of life in minoritized communities, as recognized by community organizers who appear in Chapter Five, "Access as Community Control." These organizers recognize that public school surveillance, enacted via the data that is the sine qua non of edtech, contributes to mass incarceration and the criminalization of youth—particularly youth of color (Medina Falzone, 2022), queer and trans individuals (Mountz, 2020), and/or the disabled (Nanda, 2019). As Gilmore (2007) has written, working-class and poor communities in California, multiply minoritized by race and class, find every aspect of public life drawing them toward "group-differentiated vulnerability to premature death." Working-class and poor people of color are relegated to enclosures where they are "expected, and in many ways, compelled, to sicken and so die" (Gilmore, 2017, p. 228). Gilmore sees the increasing use of prisons as part of a "carceral geography" that shapes the relations of all dispersed across it, those who end up in prisons, those who benefit from the labor extracted there, and all of us who find our own lives deformed by the "catchall solution to social problems" that is the modern prison system (p. 230).

In terms of scholarly disciplines and genres, I recognize that writing about prisons and prison abolition generally appears in venues apart from writings about human-computer interaction. Part of what I argue in this book is that, from the perspective of working-class and poor communities in Southern California, edtech and prisons are intimately related: the appeal of the former is as an exit strategy for the latter. Both Gilmore and Sojoyner use the term *enclosure* to talk about the whole complex of relations that structure life in minoritized communities in ways that perennially create less valuable, more exploitable forms of life. They both point to role of the state in maintaining these relations and the difficulty of finding a language that can capture that which is so easily obscured by accepted, well-intentioned terms like *school-to-prison pipeline* (and many other terms available from research on technology, for that matter). Access to technology appears as a progressive, technocratic undertaking, a way of addressing inequality and economic equality by affording working-class and poor students of color a path to upward mobility. But this presumptive solution depends entirely on the notion that the home communities of "urban schools" are unlivable and can only be escaped by judicious self-regulation and tech sector largesse. Edtech, surveillance, prisons, police, transit, immigration, criminal justice, gentrification, environmental degradation, and many other facets of life in minoritized communities are part of the shared experience of collective life, and people in the community have adopted virtually limitless strategies and responses to these forces. There are many facets of life in minoritized communities that do not occur strictly in response to inequality, with shared undertakings that are joyful, creative, and sophisticated. But in terms of the raced and gendered hierarchies that comprise the public sphere, people from minoritized communities share a situation shaped by policies, symbolic systems, and technologies that reaffirm, recreate, and sustain deep inequality. As Allen (2021) writes, "Race . . . like ethnicity (like gender, like nationality), is always constituted by and through particular political projects and conjunctures (everywhere)" (p. 16, parentheses in original). In what follows, I attend ethnographically to the uses of digital technology at an urban school, at a tech-focused charter management organization that manages many urban schools, and by community organizers working both with and against data. In these multiple sites, digital technology use is contextualized by larger racial projects that give life in working-class and poor communities of color a shape and hue always recognizable by those of us who come from them.

Datalogical Enframing

To center the study of racial projects in an analysis of contemporary forms of edtech is to contend with "the 'productive' (in the generic sense of producing things, not in the normative sense of necessarily beneficial) function of race within technical systems" (Benjamin, 2019, p. 105, parentheses in original). In this book, I follow Benjamin's analytical stage directions by framing as a racial project the attempts to make racially segregated public education technologically advanced and data-driven, a project capitalized on (not figuratively) by the tech sector, carried out by caring and concerned professionals, coyly subverted by some crafty individuals, and resisted at many levels by community members themselves. Racial projects figure in public education, certainly, but also in the impetus to become data-driven. In this book, I offer the analytical term *datalogical enframing* to highlight the ways that the pursuit of access to technology and the inevitable pivot to data-drivenness both support racial projects. Datalogical enframing describes those practices that justify the distribution of resources and services according to racial hierarchies via an appeal to data, data visualization, and data-drivenness. It rests on a color-blind racism that benefits organizations and individuals (as opposed to the public or the community) by producing an insatiable demand for data.

Datalogical enframing can be thought of as a certain industriousness with data that supports racial projects. In the twentieth century, educators, reformers, and government officials pursued policies inspired by Social Darwinism and other forms of race science that aimed to improve racialized subjects via deracination, or the forced shedding of culturally specific forms of speech, action, and dress in favor of supposedly neutral (i.e., white) customs (Martinez HoSang & LaBennett, 2020). At its core, datalogical enframing amounts to a similar deracination of subjects via their representation as data. I use this analytic term in what follows to link access to technology, data-drivenness, and community resistance, emphasizing throughout the great range of sentiment and complex appraisal expressed by those who live and work in the community.

Chapters 2 and 3 both draw from a field-based study I conducted from 2013 to 2015 at a South Los Angeles high school. "Access as Social Justice," the first part of this story, focuses on how a modest charter school started with an effort to expand access to technology for working-class students of color, but ultimately instrumented itself to collect and analyze data about students and teachers.[7] Over a period of two years, administrators invoked a social justice rationale to undertake an ambitious program that placed a tablet computer in the hands of every student, teacher, and administrator. This complex and labor-intensive effort involved coordinated, fundamental changes in how the school operated, including shortening instructional time, mandating the use of devices in teaching, and using student labor for maintenance. Despite the proliferation of available digital hardware and free-to-use software, instructors largely ignored the devices. School administrators, however, found many uses for the newly generated data, especially for standardized testing and discipline. In effect, the collection, aggregation, and analysis of data displaced the program's commitment to social justice and became its sole focus, in a post hoc justification that ultimately became the program's guiding principle.

In chapter 3, "Access as Surveillance," I describe how school administrators found incidental uses for data generated by mandated tablet computers by integrating it into their already extensive surveillance routines.[8] School authorities depicted their own digital surveillance capabilities as immediate, inescapable, and predictive, but as tablet computers achieved ubiquity, students and teachers challenged the ambiguous relationship between digital data and the behavior supposedly described by such data in surprising ways. Conflicts over data emerged between school authorities and targets of surveillance: students and teachers contested data-driven surveillance, revealing the control afforded by data to be partial and negotiated. Concepts from datafication show that data-intensive surveillance produces little value for the minoritized communities from which data is extracted, but legitimizes those organizations that can now claim to be data-driven. Chapter Three fleshes out the concept of datalogical enframing to show how data work by organizations can confer enormous reputational benefits on institutions, without any corresponding change with respect to their own effectiveness.

"Access as Management," the fourth chapter, zooms out to consider how data produced across urban schools in the name of empowering students through edtech directs resources out of racialized and minoritized communities.[9] This chapter tracks the aggregation, analysis, and visualization of data at a charter management organization (CMO) that manages a dozen schools in both South and East Los Angeles. Based on fieldwork conducted between 2016 and 2018, this chapter describes the ambiguity and uncertainty that data professionals working in urban education confront in the course of their work. Despite a heterogeneous set of views about the potential of such work to contribute to the improvement of public education for their Latinx and Black students, data professionals relied on a single medium to communicate their interpretations of data to school personnel and other members of the organization. A bespoke platform of 125 dashboards afforded stakeholders a graphical means of conveying objectivity, certainty, and actuarial foresight, even in cases where data professionals doubted the validity of their own analyses. Data professionals were encouraged to produce visual displays that supported the mission of the CMO and its story of racial uplift. Whether the data work touted by this organization produced better educational outcomes than other organizations was expressly beside the point: the strategy of datalogical enframing effectively removed any such question from organizational purview. This strategy allowed the organization to claim to mitigate racialized outcomes in the "intensely segregated schools" under its administration, and to simultaneously accommodate the racial project that creates, funds, and maintains them (Orfield & Jarvie, 2020).

Chapter 5, "Access as Community Control,"[10] considers how working-class communities of color respond to datafication through community organizing and public advocacy. Activists in minoritized communities have long deployed quantitative practices to argue for desired policies, draw public attention to racial inequality, and drive institutional change. Contemporary grassroots activists ironically operate amid intensified expectations about the evidentiary and communicative capacities of data—the very same expectations that give rise to the educational interventions discussed in earlier chapters. This chapter describes how community organizers working in minoritized communities negotiate this paradox. In the process, they use data as a political tool, even as they draw attention to the harms of data-intensive surveillance in public education and other sites of civic life. I reflect on how "people's community control of technology"—an amended goal of the Black Panther Party's Ten-Point Program—provides a conceptual tool for the creation of civic virtues able to speak to the interests of the multiracial working class. As the community organizers featured in this book insist, such an approach to computing would prioritize the liberatory potentials of data outside existing regimes of extraction.

This book concludes with an appeal to recommit to the civic aspirations of American public education and to decouple these goals from narratives of technological progress and data-drivenness. A broad reevaluation of the civic purposes of urban schools must first acknowledge the state's abdication of its duty to provide quality public education to minoritized communities. Without consideration of the extractions detailed in this book, the push to insert data-intensive edtech into urban schools can never contribute to racial justice or the development of a more educated, responsible citizenry. Revisiting the central argument of this book, I speculate on how we might reconfigure the resource field denoted by the term *access to technology*, not only to acknowledge the labor of teachers, students, and data professionals, but also to produce material benefits for working-class communities of color.

02 Access as Social Justice

A Cautionary Tale

In 2013, the Los Angeles Unified School District, the nations' second-largest school district by number of students, authorized the Common Core Technology Project, a highly publicized technological project that aimed to create what it boasted would be a "seismic shift" in the delivery of public education (Margolin et al., 2015). The project would outfit every student, teacher, and administrator with a tablet computer, an Apple iPad, each device equipped with a Common Core–aligned curriculum (California Department of Education, 2023) in the form of an app by the academic publisher Pearson. Local media reported that over $1.3 billion had been pledged by superintendent John Deasy to implement this tech-centric vision in the more than one thousand schools of the Los Angeles Unified School District (LAUSD); the money was to come from bonds previously approved in local elections, including funds allocated for facilities. The push to go all-in on a new standardized curriculum and a new one-to-one computer plan was touted by district public relations statements in language that married social justice concerns with tech jargon. *Time* characterized the investment as "a forward-thinking, even glamorous, way to transcend the socioeconomic barriers to academic achievement" (Pickert, 2014). A mere two years later, the LAUSD program was again profiled by national journalists, not as a marker of educational success and futurity, but as a cautionary tale. The Common Core Technology Project program flamed out in a series of spectacular missteps, breakdowns, and failures-to-launch, each humiliation covered extensively as a public scandal: bidding for the program was determined to have violated district policies and possibly state law; the Pearson app was never fully developed or distributed, leaving teachers to rely on social media, free-to-use software, or self-produced materials for instruction; the tablet computer's lack of a keyboard limited the utility of most devices for writing, note-taking, or any kind of specialized notation; and many schools lacked adequate IT support or wireless network connectivity to support an influx of bandwidth-hungry devices. Sensational rumors of gangs of dropouts roving the streets to steal tablets from students taking the bus or train to school became urban legends despite a total lack of evidence of any such crime. By 2016, Superintendent Deasy had resigned amid allegations of favoritism in bidding, his tenure ended ignominiously by the public failure of the tablet computer program. The iPad program was largely abandoned, although significant investment in digital technology across all public schools in Los Angeles continued to rise steadily, a trend intensified by the COVID-19 public health emergency.

Public failures, such as the LAUSD's iPad fiasco, are a moment ripe for social analysis. As Stalder (2002) writes, "The failed often contains the seeds of the new, and the successful is often built on the basis of the failed" (p. 218). This observation reminds us that despite whatever journalistic vicissitudes a program like the

Common Core Technology Program might endure, there is a direction and character to the incorporation of technology in public life, a long trendline that moves ever toward greater and more fundamental incorporation of digital technologies in everyday life. While the LAUSD's iPad fantasy remained largely unrealized, the marriage of social justice talk and tech jargon that made the project seem prudent—or even necessary—proved resilient, spurring new public investment in Southern California schools. The cautionary moral of the story, according to *Wired* magazine and sympathetic policymakers and academics, was not that so much money, hardware, and media attention had been drummed up by an appeal for access to technology for Los Angeles Unified students, but that needed, vital, socially just access had been implemented in the wrong way. That these particular computers had failed to contribute meaningfully to the democratically vital education of the youth of Los Angeles said nothing about the necessity of access, which maintained its spectacular self-evidence. Instead, it was schools and the humans who ran them who were to blame for failing to meet the demands of access correctly.

The Common Core Technology Project followed a predictable pattern of hype and disappointing results. Ten years earlier, Larry Cuban identified such a pattern in his studies of computers in classrooms, which he characterized as "oversold and underused" (Cuban, 2003). Cuban studied several schools varying in demographic, geographic, and economic character and observed that the introduction of computers did little to alter teaching: most teachers ignored computers and stuck to the instructional routines and techniques they knew best. Moreover, student use of computing resources could not be correlated to any positive change in any accepted measurement of learning (e.g., standardized test scores, grades, graduation rates). In short, investments in technology had succeeded in making computers widespread in classrooms but had not produced measurable improvements in learning. Cuban's interest was primarily in the long history of education reform in the United States, how the belief in public schools as the bedrock of a democratic society impelled continuous, successive waves of policy changes and counterchanges. While Cuban left open the question of whether or not classroom computers might someday fulfill their promise, his work implied that classroom technology was a powerful agent of reform that might, someday, meet a counterreform of its own, a force that would unsettle common assumptions about education and augur new kinds of institutional and professional arrangements. At present, such counterreform has largely failed to materialize, especially in those so-called urban schools that serve minoritized communities, including the schools of interest to the next three chapters of this book. With the benefit of hindsight, Cuban's work looks more like evidence that digital technologies themselves are a kind of superficial reform all to themselves.[1]

Still, at the same moment a public failure surprising for its speed and intensity (if not its narrative arc) unfolded, roughly five miles due south of LAUSD's downtown headquarters, another school district accomplished what proved so elusive elsewhere in the city. Academy Schools, a public charter management organization (CMO) that runs approximately twenty-five middle and high schools, pursued a program nearly identical to the larger LAUSD's Common Core Technology Project. Mirroring LAUSD's highly publicized efforts, Academy schools ordered the principals of their roughly dozen high schools to institute a one-to-one program, one that would also give each student, teacher, and administrator an iPad and a Common Core–aligned app developed by Pearson.

I was introduced by a friend who taught at an Academy school to his boss, Principal Dan Montoya of Academy Schools Preparatory School Number Seven (all academy schools are referred to by number, until the name of the school is changed to honor a notable Academy personality, such as a large donor). After he learned that my family came from South Los Angeles and that I was a first-gen grad student working on a doctorate at UCLA, Principal Montoya agreed to host an open-ended research project based on Number Seven's experience with tablets. Later that week, I was invited to a faculty meeting to pitch my project and ask teachers for their cooperation. Principal Montoya and his staff gave me permission to visit the school as frequently as I liked, provided that I did not interfere with any school activity. As a courtesy, I asked teachers for permission to enter their classrooms, but only once did a teacher deny me entry to a classroom for any reason (she invited me to return later the same day). For two consecutive school years, I visited Number Seven regularly, logging approximately 275 hours inside the school. I watched classes, attended faculty meetings, recorded interviews, and examined devices and documents. Outside of school hours, I went to sponsored extracurricular events such as meetings of student groups and games of some of the school's sports teams. I also took part in social events, such as the school renaming ceremony (detailed in the next chapter), prom, and graduation. I corresponded with teachers and administrators via text and email. I joined students for service activities, such as a health fair at the Catholic church across the street and a beach cleanup at Dockweiler State Beach. I also attended special events in the community, such as a computers class for parents organized jointly by the school and the local library. After hours, I visited with teachers in coffee shops, bars, and their homes. I met with parents at the school or in the neighborhood. I once taught a lesson for a science teacher who had fallen ill too suddenly to get a substitute. I served as a community volunteer in the school's annual exit interviews for graduating seniors (the kids dressed up and brought in real résumés to apply for fictional jobs). I became especially close with a group called Student Technology Leaders (STLs), originally a club for students interested in learning about computers. Principal Montoya left the school during the third year of the project, at which point my permission to visit the school was immediately terminated by his successor, Vice Principal Gomez.

This chapter tells the first part of a story about access and how the language of social justice coexists with and supports the extraction of resources (including time, labor, and data) from the minoritized communities that access to computing is supposed to benefit. After a period of unrest and novelty, where many problems reminiscent of the larger LAUSD's misadventure with tablet computers occurred, Number Seven was able to do what the larger public school district could not: a copycat program successfully distributed a tablet computer to each student, teacher, and administrator in a busy, bustling, South Los Angeles public high school. Over a period of two years, administrators explicitly invoked social justice to explain why they had undertaken such a complex and labor-intensive effort, arguing that the provision of access to computing resources was itself a needed form of social justice, irrespective of whatever kinds of teaching and learning these resources might enable. They married this talk of social justice to other rationales, including talk about the future, about markets, and about education. Like other kinds of organizations, schools speak in many voices, the interplay of which reveals the complex dynamics at work in corporate speech (Seaver, 2017): administrators, teachers and even students frequently invoked social justice in describing the tablet program, but they also frequently talked about competition, the future, computing itself, life in the 'hood. School administrators frequently described access as a way of instilling in students a certain kind of facility or literacy with technology beyond what could be measured by conventional assessments, a kind of "value add" that came on top of the standard high school curriculum. The point here is that tablets arrived without any single, coherent policy justification and sat comfortably within many contradictory ways of thinking about schooling and technology. Tablets were viewed by students and administrators as fun, beneficial, and needed, a rare case of youth and authority figures coming to complete agreement. But whatever rhetorical justifications might circulate at any given moment, the tablet computer program had *material* consequences, including shortened instructional time, the establishment of formal rules that mandated tablets in teaching, and extensive reliance on uncompensated student labor for routine maintenance and IT work. After a painful period of trial and error, Number Seven came up with a workaround to manage the support, maintenance, and IT labor needed to keep hundreds of new computing devices charged, updated, connected, and secured. Number Seven settled upon a way of doing access that avoided any of the accusations of failure that beset LAUSD's project, but this success with tablet computers came at significant cost in terms of time, labor, and data. The primary outcome of this effort matches what Cuban and other researchers have long diagnosed: despite the proliferation of available digital hardware and free-to-use software, instructors largely ignored these devices. In other words, access was accomplished at great cost, but such access did not deliver promised benefits, including promises of high-tech learning or social justice.

First Day of School

On November 18, 2013, after several weeks of intense and sometimes frantic planning, staging, and troubleshooting, Principal Montoya, his three assistant principals, and Sonia Quezada, a math teacher recruited to serve as manager of technology, supervised the distribution of over five hundred iPads to students in grades nine through eleven in a day-long event that displaced all instruction (seniors were given devices later in the school year). Principal Montoya and his staff undertook a number of preparations prior to the distribution of the devices to make sure that their one-to-one program was uncontroversial. Most of these activities concerned the integrity of the devices themselves: where they would be stored, how they would be counted, where they would be connected to electrical outlets. Principal Montoya held a series of mandatory meetings for parents early in the school year, wherein a legal guardian was required to sign forms authorizing a student's participation. Parents were not provided any opportunity to opt out of this agreement. Ms. Quezada produced and distributed a ten-page "Student Acceptable Use Policy" that all students in the school also signed; it read like a terms of service agreement. The LAUSD program, barely three months old, was already mired in controversy.[2]

Ms. Quezada was the teacher I worked most closely with during my field work. She was Salvadoran American, the daughter of immigrants who had settled in Southern California in the 1980s. Her father had worked with computers, instilling in Ms. Quezada in interest in technology. Ms. Quezada taught mostly remedial Algebra courses, which many of the students needed in order to graduate. She considered herself an expert in technology and had worked for many years as faculty advisor for the STL program; Principal Montoya delegated anything to do with technology to her, although she drew no additional pay for this work. For years she had run after-school clubs and summer programs for students who wanted to learn more about computing: it was her passion, and her greatest professional goal was to teach an AP computer science course. In her work with the STLs, Ms. Quezada saw herself passing along a hobby that could also be a useful life skill. As the mother of a teen, she rarely bothered to feign professional disinterest in her students. She called all her kids (and me) by affectionate nicknames instead of our individual names: sweetheart, honey, mijo.

The day of the distribution of the iPads, many invited guests came to observe the rollout. Higher-ups from home office, officials from other schools interested in implementing one-to-one programs of their own, teachers from sister Academy schools, journalists, esteemed graduates, and a few researchers (myself included) joined the staff and students of Number Seven for the day to watch a tightly scripted routine that ended with each student in possession of a tablet computer. Specially appointed "student ambassadors" roamed the halls, greeted guests, offered directions helpfully, and invited those interested to observe classes in session. The elaborate production, coordinated by Ms. Quezada and that cadre of her STLs, involved nearly every student, teacher, and administrator in the school at some point. Students spent all day in their advisories (a noninstructional homeroom period largely dedicated to administrative work), waiting for a turn to get their hands on the iPads that had been delivered to the school a few weeks earlier and stored in a locked classroom. Class by class, students came to Room 109, commandeered for the day from Ms. Wilson, whose Language Arts classes would be canceled for the duration, to line up and receive a device in its sleek, white, Apple packaging. The room was divided up into stations so that each student could cycle through to check out a tablet and get a standard-issue carrying case, required by the student contract (Figure 1). Ms. Quezada described the setup, designed and executed by her STLs, as being "just like the DMV." Just as details of the implementation of the iPad program had been delegated to school principals by the home office, the burden of clerical, inventory control, and IT work was likewise shifted, this time to students, especially the STLs. The STLs presided over what was a powerfully analog process. The paper-intensive procession, stage-directed by a list called "Station Assignments," enumerated each STL's name underneath a brief description of his or her responsibility and a scripted statement or action. Check the ID. Check the signature. File the form. Update the database.

To begin, each advisory class lined up in the hall outside Room 109. Each student brought in a signed pink slip of paper, the signature page of the " Student Acceptable Use Policy," and stood at a piece of blue tape on the floor marked "STOP! WAIT HERE." STLs policed the lines to control the physical position and placement of waiting students as if it were a game of "Mother May I." STLs gleefully sent students back to retrieve missing paperwork, a move that deliberately shamed the unprepared student, brought the distribution to a halt, and deterred onlookers from violating protocol. There were rare hiccups, caused by students who had been absent on a critical day or who had only started at the school in the previous day or two, but as planned, the STLs were able to issue every eligible student an iPad inside the span of a single school day. They marked their best time for processing a class on the wall and

FIGURE 1. iPad checkout, directed by Student Technology Leaders. November 18, 2013. Photo by author.

made a game out of trying to beat the number. Ms. Tonya Watson, Academy's director of innovation and technology, showed off the work of the industrious STLs to a reporter. Speaking to an ad hoc cluster of five or six observers, she proudly boasted that a full 100 percent of parents had agreed to have their students participate by signing the contract and thereby assuming financial responsibility for the tablets. The habitual bells and public addresses sounded throughout the day, announcing lunch, directing movements, and providing on-the-fly rule changes: "Students must use the outside staircase only at this time" or "Teachers, use the PowerPoint mailed to you by Ms. Quezada this morning. Disregard all other emails."

After a given advisory got its iPads, pairs of STLs went to that advisory classroom to instruct students how to set up the devices using a detailed presentation that included a PowerPoint and a text called "iPad Setup Script for Students." STLs guided the entire setup process: I watched an STL (Layla O.) guide a class through turning on the iPad, connecting to the school's network, and opening an app for the first time. She stood at the front of the room in high-heeled shoes and spoke confidently, advancing her PowerPoint presentation from a laptop at the lectern, deftly answering questions. Another STL, Pablo, went around the room to troubleshoot individual devices. The teacher of the advisory, Ms. Digiorno, was not directly involved in any of these processes; she chatted with other visitors to the class and directed all questions to the STLs. As she delivered her presentation, Layla O. twice admonished the group, "Remember: this is a tool, not a toy," a mantra printed in the training materials. After the presentation, Layla O. and Pablo left to go guide another advisory through setup: they were booked solid all day. In parting, Layla O. reminded students that the iPads were subject to inspection and specifically warned that the school would "keep surveillance" over activity on the devices. Ms. Digiorno then had the students go through a self-guided list of forty-two activities called "Getting to know your iPad" that included reading the battery display, opening apps, copying text, and taking screenshots. I asked Ms. Digiorno how she thought the new tablets would help with instruction and, before she could answer, one of her students chimed in: "It'll be a distraction."

Throughout the entire day, teachers, students, and administrators talked about what they thought the tablets would do. The visiting executive from Academy Schools, Ms. Watson, talked about how the tablets would help "close the achievement gaps." She used this talking point a few times for different groups of visitors, clearly expert in both media communications and education research. Principal Montoya appeared pleased that all the devices made it into students' hands and that so many people had turned out to see what a successful program looked like. Ms. Quezada darted about frantically with a walkie-talkie in one hand and her cellphone in another, shouting orders to her STLs. Mr. Michaels, an electives teacher and chair of the student council, described the distribution as exhibiting the best qualities of Number Seven and Academy Schools. As he explained it, it was the school's job as an organization to be "at the cutting edge." He described the school's activities as always defined by two directives: to pursue social justice through education and to serve the organization, "a one-two punch." He described the goal of educating and inspiring students as the mission of the school and invoked the liberal arts as an example of this directive. In this respect, the iPad program would put "information at their [students'] fingertips." The second imperative, of equal importance, was business. He described the school as market-driven, as operating under a business paradigm: "We get results that justify what we do here. This program will get results. It will have to."

The first episode of so-called *hacking*, any unauthorized use of a device, took place almost immediately. A student gained the ability to download apps by changing the time and date settings on his iPad. Based on the instructions he found on a website, he installed a videogame on his tablet. Rumors of the video game hack circulated quickly: students used their school-issued tablets and their own smartphones to get the word out. An STL alerted Ms. Quezada of the violation, who in turn informed Principal Montoya. The offending student and his iPad were summoned to Ms. Quezada's room so that she could determine how the hack had defeated the school's network and device security. Ms. Quezada's monitoring software could not detect the unapproved software. Exhausted from the intense day's labor, she repeated in frustration, "I can't see it," meaning that the interface of her monitoring software (an enterprise-level device management platform called the Casper Suite, later renamed Jamf Pro) could not detect the noneducational software on the individual device. From her interface, the offending tablet appeared only to have the standard set of apps installed, although by physically inspecting the tablet, she could see an icon for the game on the home screen. Principal Montoya informed the offending student that he would be punished for violating the student contract—"hacking" being an infringement potentially punishable by expulsion—but that the punishment would be suspended as long as he did not tell anyone else how to install unauthorized games.

A short time later, just minutes after the last advisory had started their self-guided tour of the iPad, another announcement came over the PA system. Vice Principal Tustin, director of instruction and student success, said, "All right, teachers: it is now time to make sure all your students' iPads are locked up at this time." At this command, advisory teachers instructed their students to place their iPads inside a designated charging cart, a sort of wheeled safe, that had been placed in every advisory classroom. STLs called roll in each room so that every student present could check back in his or her iPad. No sooner had the STLs completed the work of getting every student a tablet, than they were called upon to lock them up for the day: to minimize the risk of loss, theft, or damage, Principal Montoya and the home office had decided that the students' tablets could not leave the school. STLs spread out in their teams to show teachers how to secure tablets at the end of the school day and dedicated a full hour to assuring that every single iPad issued that day was accounted for and locked inside its designated cart. A month would pass before students were again allowed to touch the devices, during which time the STLs used what they had learned that day to perfect their inventory routine. They drilled constantly over the month to create and master new sets of procedures to handle inventory: regular check-out, fire drill check-in, early release, and so forth.

The first day of school for tablet computers was an aberration, an exceptional day in a school culture that values routine. Sims's (2017) term *sanctioned counterpractices* is useful here: such authorized deviations from routine help people in the school feel united around a purpose and a sense of novelty, but they are easily incorporated into the day-in and day-out grind, much like a pep rally or a field trip. Although the iPad distribution was partly a spectacle, a canny display put on to make Academy schools seem more technologically sophisticated and organizationally competent than other public schools, almost all the important patterns that I would later see with regard to this one-to-one program were on display that day: elaborate rituals around the use of tablets, little use of tablets in instruction, invocations of surveillance, contests over allowable use of computing resources between students and authorities, and a constant, unspoken game of one-upmanship with other kinds of public schools, especially the LAUSD, whose presence shadowed every decision of the school administration.

Failure Is Not an Option

Los Angeles Academy Schools Preparatory School Number Seven is located in a neighborhood called South Park. The number of students in the school varies, largely due to transfers in and out by individual students, but is usually between five hundred and six hundred. In the 2013–2014 academic year, the first year of my field work, Number Seven reported a student population that was 89 percent Latinx, 10 percent African American, and less than 1 percent white, Asian, or Native American. Most students at the school come from Spanish-speaking homes in South Los Angeles: 98 percent of students at the school qualified for free lunch that year and nearly 89 percent spoke a language other than English in the home, important metrics that education researchers and sociologists use to analyze socioeconomic status. The families of students must complete an application to apply, a four-page document that collects demographic data about the family and the student as well as education history. Before they can be admitted, students (and their parents or guardians) must agree to the terms of attendance, including rules about expectations for parental involvement, the right for the school to require additional courses for students (such as afterschool or weekend tutoring), extensive codes for behavior and dress, as well as punishments for infractions.

The faculty consists of roughly thirty credentialed full-time teachers, each of whom has completed or is in the process of completing masters-level education and professional certification in a particular subject (e.g., language arts, math, social studies). The instructional staff is joined by three full-time guidance counselors based in the school's counseling center and various part-time mental health and specialty therapy service providers who visit on a regular basis (e.g., a speech therapist who divides her week between several different schools). The administrative staff consists of the school's principal and three assistant principals, as well as a half-dozen employees whose work does not directly support instruction, such as an accountant, three security guards, and a porter. Turnover of staff at charter schools is relatively high compared to traditional public schools (Bickmore & Sulentic Dowell, 2019):

unlike LAUSD teachers, Academy schools' faculty lack the many forms of job protection or reward for seniority found in LAUSD and other unionized public school districts across California. The faculty is more racially heterogenous than the student body: roughly half of the teaching staff identified as white, while the remaining staff identified as Latinx, Black, Asian, and/or multiracial. Many of the teachers I talked to, especially those who were white or Asian, described their motivation for working at Number Seven (as opposed to any other school) in terms of commitment to social justice. It's important to note that the racial self-identification of faculty at the school embodies a dynamic where those who are racialized as white hold greater authority and expertise over those parents, students, and teachers who are not, a contested but persistent criticism of urban schools that emerges from organizational theory and education research (Knaus, 2014; Ray, 2019).

South Park is a part of the South Los Angeles region, the largest division of the city of Los Angeles; regional and national media often use the term South-Central Los Angeles as a blanket term to specify the Black and Latinx parts of the city south of the Santa Monica Freeway. South Park, Los Angeles, is a lower-income, primarily Latinx neighborhood. According to a neighborhood-by-neighborhood census data analysis by the *Los Angeles Times* Data Desk, the neighborhood is 78.6 percent Latinx and 19.2 percent Black (*Los Angeles Times* Data Desk, 2009). Relative to the Los Angeles metro area as a whole, South Park is demographically homogenous, consisting almost entirely of Latinx and Black residents. The median household income of $29,518 is low for both the city and the county. The population density and the ratio of single-parent families are among the highest in the city and county; average age and educational attainment are among the lowest. Academy

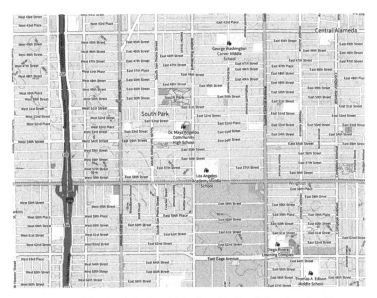

MAP 1. Map of the South Park neighborhood in South Los Angeles. Map created at OpenStreetMap (openstreetmap.org/copyright), licensed under the Creative Commons Attribution-ShareAlike 2.0 license (CC BY-SA 2.0).

Schools exclusively serves communities like South Park in terms of race and class: all of their schools in Los Angeles are located in poor and working-class communities of color, Latinx and Black neighborhoods in South and East Los Angeles.

Los Angeles has more charter schools than any other U.S. city. Across all types of charter schools, researchers have not found any specific generalizable, measurable educational benefit to this form of school organization over traditional public schools (i.e., common schools) (Lauen et al., 2015). As an independent charter, a new school opened with little administrative support or supervision from LAUSD and managed by an independent, not-for-profit organization, Number Seven represents a certain vision of

American public education reform, one based on conspicuous disciplinary regimes, meritocratic discourse, responsibilization, and market-based forms of competition in the provision of social services (Baude et al., 2014; Buras, 2014; Gawlik, 2012). Charter management organizations such as Academy Schools operate autonomously from the publicly elected board of the Los Angeles Unified School District and enjoy considerable latitude in managing the schools in their portfolios, including the exclusive use of nonunion labor and latitude to experiment with education technology. Owing to the presence of many other school districts within the region, both Academy schools and the LAUSD serve student populations that are poorer than the city as a whole: many students in wealthier (and whiter) enclaves have their own schools and school districts, such as the Beverly Hills Unified School District or the Santa Monica–Malibu Unified School District. This peculiarity of Los Angeles, coupled with the extreme racial segregation of many neighborhoods, has made charter schools commonplace, especially for working-class students of color. Whatever their merits, charter schools are a popular form of school organization in Los Angeles, especially for working-class Black and Latinx students (Frankenberg et al., 2010).

Social justice talk animated teachers' work lives: most of the students, teachers, and administrators I met talked about social justice easily, generally describing it as a way to evaluate the consequences of individual and collective action, but also as a kind of tradition that linked historical figures such as Martin Luther King Jr., Cesar Chavez, Harvey Milk, and Malala Yousafzai, all of whom were depicted in a mural on the side of the school. But social justice talk was not limited to a sort of affirmation of shared purpose among the school community; it was also deployed in more official, bureaucratic modes. Academy School's funding to buy tablet computers came from grants from nonprofit organizations and state and federal agencies. The grant applications used to fund the CMO's one-to-one program explicitly used the language of social justice to describe the need for access among the youth Academy serves. According to these documents, the program aimed to increase the college preparedness of students and to encourage underrepresented racial groups to pursue science, technology, engineering, and math (STEM) majors in college.

Social justice talk couched in term of access took the place of more recognized educational concepts such as curriculum, learning outcomes, literacy, or skills. The one-to-one program as a whole was largely improvised: only one teacher in the school reported getting any training in how to use tablets in class instruction. As research would predict, tablet computers did not radically change classroom instruction routines. Students used tablets for reference questions, looking at documents, or spontaneous activities between formal lessons, but teachers largely relied on analog media for coursework. By contrast, the administration found many uses for tablet computers in instituting disciplinary measures including extensive surveillance and expansion of standardized testing (which will be the subject of the next chapter). One-to-one laptop programs have not reliably demonstrated improved outcomes in terms of college matriculation or STEM uptake, although some studies have shown "positive improvements" in student writing or technology-based skills (Penuel, 2006). No comparable research base has yet emerged on the use of tablet computers in one-to-one programs in American primary and secondary education, although my research would support the argument that school-issued tablet computers such as the Apple iPad are probably less useful in high school education than other kinds of computing devices such as laptop computers with keyboards.

"Mass User-Unfriendliness"

At Number Seven, leadership's dictate to "do tablets" better than the Los Angeles Unified School District fell to the STLs, the same elite group of uncompensated student IT workers who directed the distribution. Through a variety of creative workarounds and clever improvisations, these student IT workers oversaw the daily distribution, inventory, and maintenance of hundreds of tablet computing devices. STL work fluctuated in terms of its technical sophistication, from recording information about devices into paper documents one day, to configuring enterprise-level security settings on the school's device management platform the next, to repairing malfunctioning tablets over the weekend. This work was varied, unceasing, and fast-paced.

Imagine for a moment a fairly routine task: viewing a PDF file. For most individual users, this would involve trivial steps such as turning on a device, connecting it to the wireless network, downloading a document, and finally, loading this document into some environment where its contents could be displayed. Now imagine this same activity scaled up by the access of thirty or so student users and one teacher, all of them attempting to perform this same task. Every step of a routine operation becomes problem-prone at this scale: thirty times the passwords, thirty times the network connections, thirty times the potential diversions, thirty times the misfingering of virtual keys, and thirty times the mandatory updates. A forgotten password or five, a tablet or three stuck on the log-in screen. A missing document, an out-of-date app, and so on, such that the management of access becomes a kind of demand. As opposed to a straightforward experience wherein a single user manipulates a single tablet, the eventual configuration of access at Number Seven took on drastically different dynamics. Disruptions were by no means uncommon; to the contrary, they were quotidian, ubiquitous, unceasing, a deep mismatch between individual users and the needs of classrooms that Ms. Quezada termed "mass user-unfriendliness."

During the first year of the tablet program, almost all of the problems that LAUSD experienced happened at Number Seven. The school's wireless network could not accommodate so many new connections and frequently went down. The device management system was complex and frequently frustrated teachers' or students' attempts to install software needed for teaching and learning: teachers could not be sure that a given app or website would be available for a lesson, so they were hesitant to rely on tablets in planning instruction.

Clever students found many ways to circumvent device security. The presence of smartphones proved especially vexing. If a teacher asked a student to look up an education resource on a tablet, the teacher had to be prepared for a deluge of complaints from students that they could not reach the resource, followed by a flood of requests to use personal smartphones to reach the same resource. This near-daily occurrence put the teaching staff in an awkward position: they had to demand that students use the partially functional iPad that the school had supplied, but also had to threaten disciplinary action if students took out the fully functional smartphone that virtually all of them owned (I never met a student who did not have a smartphone in all my years at the school, although a student would probably not readily admit to such a lack).

Perhaps unsurprisingly, managing hundreds of new devices required the management of hundreds of new cables. Managing cables turned out to be nearly as labor-intensive as managing the tablet computers themselves. Costly cables needed to be counted and controlled to make sure that no student or teacher took one home, but they also had to be reconnected to a device and a live, functioning source of electricity at the end of every day. Aside from the tablets and their armored charging carts, classrooms were already full of electronic equipment, including laptops, desktops, projectors, smart boards, and other powered accessories. In most classrooms, each outlet was taken up by some kind of expansion device (e.g., a power strip), but even so, teachers struggled to find places to charge devices that they needed for instruction. Students themselves were forbidden from plugging anything in at school for fear of producing too much competition for available outlets. Aside from being a focus of significant labor, the outlet and cable problems demonstrate the many logistical details that had to be resolved after tablets arrived and the great skill and creativity of the STLs and Ms. Quezada in doing so. More experienced IT staff might have foreseen such complications, but the STLs operated mostly through trial and error.

By spring of the first year, after a series of setbacks, difficulties, and reorganizations, the STLs and Ms. Quezada developed routines and procedures to get tablets into the hands of students every morning and back into their armored charging bays in the afternoon. The most important change was organizational: the STLs went from being an afterschool club to being a permanent volunteer workforce. The STLs became so adept at providing support for the tablet computer program that their labor became infrastructural, receding almost completely into the background and

FIGURE 2. Cables! STLs managed an analog system of paper, stickers, clipboards, and cables to support digital devices in classrooms. The management of carts, spreadsheets, stickers, and all manner of non-digital stuff also demanded student labor. Photo by author.

becoming invisible, relied upon, taken for granted (Bowker et al., 2010). During the two years of this fieldwork, none of the roughly six hundred tablet computers eventually issued were lost, stolen, or irreparably damaged, largely because of the constant work of the STLs.

The ongoing accomplishment of access—that is to say, the addition of hundreds of tablet computers to the already complex and frenetic environment of a Los Angeles public high school— proved chaotic and laborious. Yet, by the end of the second year, the devices had achieved the status of the mundane, the conflict and difficulties they had inspired in the work of teachers and students largely absorbed into the rhythms of school life. Tablets accomplished the feat of receding into the background, such that teachers and students became inured to their novelty and accustomed to the various demands they made. As Ms. Quezada put it when referring to student attitudes about the use of devices in school: "The novelty of the iPad wears off within a couple of days and so they grow almost unappreciative of technology. It's just another thing to them. They don't see it as a tool, they don't see it as a privilege. They almost desensitize to technology."

The story of Number Seven's experience with tablet computers centers on contestation, conflict, and eventual détente around access. To reach this point, a considerable amount of largely unanticipated tech support work had to be completed, work that turned a novel, highly anticipated technology into "just another thing." To maintain this thing-ness, teachers and administrators delegated a great deal of work to STLs. STLs did not receive pay or class credit for their work. In a written activity we did together, these students reported spending an average of three hours per day doing tablet-related work and occasionally came in over vacation or on weekends. STLs developed systems to count, store, charge, repair, and configure student tablets, a set of duties that had to be planned, executed, and routinized in response to the demands posed by access.

In addition to spontaneous episodes of support, STLs performed regular, extensive, time-sensitive duties including a daily inventory of tablet computers. The protocol of the inventory evolved over the first year, ultimately taking the following form: during the afternoon advisory class, pairs of STLs assigned to each classroom supervised the placement of tablets into armored carts; STLs maintained one such cart in each advisory class. The school's principals patrolled the halls with walkie-talkies, monitoring the process. STLs unlocked each cart and returned every student tablet to its indexed slot inside, secured a charging cable to each device, and checked for damage to the unit, the cable, or the protective case. After the STLs had completed a checklist assuring that every tablet in their care had been successfully located, they locked the cart and hung a green card from the lintel of the advisory classroom's doorway. Should STLs discover a tablet missing in a room, they would hang a red card from the lintel and alert the principal who would issue an order to lock down the school. During lockdown, all the school's entrances and exits were sealed, and all students and teachers remained in classrooms until the missing device was located. I witnessed the lockdown protocol twice, although each time it turned out that a missing tablet had been mislaid in the building, once by an assistant principal and once by a student heading off-campus for a game. These false alarms did little to puncture the tremendous energies that school administration spent on combatting thefts, which were never once confirmed by media, police, or school officials (Blume, 2013). Extensive security measures at

FIGURE 3. Ms. Quezada took this picture of the armored charging carts lined up in the upstairs hallway in advance of their installation in each classroom; she followed with a text that said, "mass user-unfriendliness." Photo by Ms. Quezada.

Number Seven were entirely successful at preventing loss, and few teachers or students questioned the necessity of such an elaborate pageant of security work, of the colored flags and spot inspections, the shrill static of walkie-talkies audible in classrooms.

Access required the expansion of a noninstructional class period in the afternoon, used exclusively for the collection, inspection, and counting of tablets by designated pairs of STLs. While an additional twelve minutes per day spent in noninstructional classes might seem trivial, this administrative adjustment resulted in a reduction of thirty-six hours of instructional time over the whole school year. Demonstrating neatly the action of information technology on the perception of time, the putatively trivial demands of the tablets themselves reconfigured some of the terms of classroom instruction and, as a result, renegotiated the fundamental terms upon which public education as practiced by Number Seven operated. Such action defies one of the CMO's previously stated priorities, listed in its own promotional materials as one of the four "core values" that distinguish its model of education: "increased instructional time." Access demanded this time, a resource that had already been allocated for other purposes, according to other values. In the rush of daily life, this profoundly symbolic and materially significant change was absorbed into the cyclical ebb and flow of assignments, tests, assemblies, conferences, and meetings, the bureaucratic ups and downs of every school year.

Students' work on the tablets involved the manipulation of many forms of information. Mobile technologies such as smartphones and tablets feature, by design, a short product life cycle and a reliance on frequent software updates (Farman, 2017). In this way, tablets frequently demanded digital information in the form of software updates. STLs performed many kinds of ancillary informational tasks in a variety of media, including recordkeeping, labeling, and scheduling. Downloading and installing major updates, for example, had to be coordinated, timed, and executed in ways that would not interrupt access. Synchronizing such an update with teaching schedules, class calendars, and so on to assure the continuity of access required the creation of documents

FIGURE 4. A pair of STLs returning a cart full of tablets to a classroom. The STLs came in over the summer to help Ms. Quezada get the tablets ready for school. Photo by author.

to track these occurrences. In addition to these largely digital documentary demands, students had to manage analog documents, especially in connection to upkeep of the locking carts where tablets were stored when not in use. Much of the management of tablets depended on the manipulation or provision of analog and digital information: files to be transferred, forms to be filled, notes to be written, receipts to be traded, and paperwork to be signed.

The physical presence of tablets was merely the leading edge of a "working configuration" of numerous resources (Suchman, 1996). In a reversal, students themselves were required to provide information demanded by the management of tablets and the various apps, platforms, and publishers that provided educational media. Local rules, legal contracts, terms of service agreements, and technical protocols multiplied, making demands for information in specific material forms. These documentary obligations were attended to largely through the labor of uncompensated students. Such documentary demands complicate the frequently touted vision of a "paperless office," one sometimes invoked by administrators to justify the tablet computer program (Gitelman, 2014, p. 128). In this example, access becomes a quid pro quo, an exchange of information at one site for the promise of its delivery elsewhere.

The provision of these resources amounted to the continual transformation of the unwaged labor of students and the devices themselves into a configuration called access. This analysis underscores the complexity of the constant labors needed to keep access, a dynamic that does not figure in a general claim of the social justice virtues of digital technologies. The resources that kept tablets in a predictable, stable condition available for classroom use were not inconsequential. As one student worker wrote,

Student Technology Leaders has been difficult in some ways in my schoolwork because there are some days where I get pulled out of class to do some work and when this happens, I lose some learning time. Then I get behind with my work and sometimes the teachers teach new material that I have to come back to later, such as after school, so I can ask her what I missed. This takes time off of other things.

Elsewhere, I have written more extensively about how students themselves accounted for the benefits and costs of iPad use in their school (Crooks, 2019). Unsurprisingly, STLs were intensely aware of the extreme demands on their time and energy made by unwaged, uncompensated work. But, as they reflected on all they had done, the overwhelming majority of STLs agreed that the program had been worthwhile for them. They enjoyed the prominence and social capital that being in the STL program gave them, as well as the greater freedom and autonomy from day-to-day schoolwork that the position afforded. Their endorsement was guarded and deliberately ambivalent, another kind of cautionary tale that focused on how someone has to pay to maintain access for others via time, labor, stress, and energy. Still, given the chance to do it over, all the STLs I spoke with said that they would sign up for the program again, even knowing in advance how demanding it would be. This evaluation scandalized me at the time, shocked my sense of fairness that so much free labor should go to maintain a form of access that was rarely used in instruction and had little to do with the social justice claims that motivated the tablet program in the beginning. But the STLs were not naive: they understood better than I did that working with technology can confer reputational benefits. Even if the claims that boosters of a technology make are complete nonsense, the clout is real.

Technology Is the Whole Point

What is access for? Why would a school in a poorer community in Los Angeles hang its hopes for students on something as untested and relatively expensive as a tablet computer, especially given a relatively clear research record that would contraindicate such an intervention? The point of the program was not a means to accomplish something (such as an improvement in test scores or graduation rates) but was an end unto itself: to use technology.

That Academy schools should so closely monitor and respond to programs in schools outside of its own organizational control initially surprised me, but public education in Los Angeles, especially for working-class Black and Latinx students in South L.A. and East L.A., has long been marked by competition between charter schools and traditionally managed public schools. So part of what access to technology meant at Number Seven had more to do with an association with the tech sector, an attempt to burnish its own reputation through the use of digital technology. This appeal to the reputation of technology was, from the perspective of school leadership, at least half of the reason for "doing tablets" in the first place. As some savvy teachers and students described it, competition within L.A. schools and the need to distinguish their technological superiority was the entire point of the program. Given these overwhelming and overdetermining imperatives, success with technology was mandatory. CMO leadership demanded success from principals, who in turn demanded it from teachers, who in turn demanded it form STLs. Moreover, success had a fairly narrow definition that meant, in effect, "Don't break or lose an expensive tablet computer."

These very different commitments, social justice versus competition, spoke to the realpolitik of work in charter schools in Los Angeles, the reality that charter schools themselves ideologically and financially challenge the broader school system without confronting the racial segregation that characterizes public education in Southern California (and in most school districts in the United States) (Orfield et al., 2016). Charter school operators such as Academy Schools do not contest or even address this inequality. Instead, they offer the value proposition that they can mitigate the negative consequences of racially segregated public schooling through superior techniques and facility with technology.

Ultimately, the rationale for the tablet computer program also receded into the background as the devices became a vector for something else entirely, something not originally part of the high-minded promises that accompanied their arrival: school administrators quickly realized that, whatever their utility in instruction, tablet computers could be used to capture data about students and teachers. Technology adopted for the betterment of students could also be used to monitor, sort, and discipline. In contrast to coming up with practical ways to incorporate hundreds of new computing devices in face-to-face teaching, administrators had no difficulty devising ways to make tablets useful in extending various forms of surveillance. The tactics that administrators deployed to try to monitor, sort, and control teachers and students spawned many contradictions in terms of what authorities imagined data could tell them and what their surveillance powers could actually accomplish, but in the end, these regimes of surveillance were productive. It turned out that, for the organization, using tablet computers to capture data in support of administrative priorities had nothing to do with any particular capacity of statistical or computational analysis. This dynamic, the way that faulty, spurious, or absent relationships in data could be turned into practical benefits is another aspect of what I call *datalogical enframing*.

Public charter schools like Academy schools accommodate the larger racial project of distributing quality public education according to racial hierarchies. Datalogical enframing trains the organization's vision only on individual behavior, preemptively locking out of view any data analysis that might describe how the reality of school segregation affects impacted students, families, or communities. This strategy allows the organization to make students, families, and even teachers responsible for optimizing the outputs of an educational system that is inherently, intentionally, and relentlessly unequal. Moreover, many kinds of resources are captured via student computing at a variety of levels. In particular, inserting computing devices into schools produces a glut of digital data, data that can be captured and acted on by those parties with the acumen and skills to make use of it. Regrettably, that does not generally include the community whose needs occasioned access in the first place.

03 Access as Surveillance

Every person in the system is held accountable for student success and uses data to appraise improvement efforts.

ACADEMY SCHOOLS, Overview

Accountability Stories

In 2014, at the start of the second year of my fieldwork, after the school had, in the words of Ms. Quezada, "turned a corner" with respect to newly available tablet computers, wealthy donors, through charitable giving, secured naming rights at Number Seven. Academy Schools Preparatory School Number Seven would be rechristened in honor of these patrons: starting in December, Number Seven became known as Academy Charles and Carol Peterson Leadership School. The letterhead, the website, the sign out front: all of it had to be changed to mark the commitment from the Petersons, who had pledged $1 million to Academy Schools. Principal Montoya's staff mailed out invitations weeks in advance to invite members of state and local government, reporters, school advocates, parents, and representatives from both Los Angeles

Unified School District and Academy Schools to a renaming ceremony in the courtyard, followed by a buffet lunch of beans and rice served in the parking lot across the street. Students were instructed to dress in formal uniform: polo shirts that indicated grade rank by color, khaki pants—no shorts or sneakers. The ceremony took place on December 5, 2014, but for weeks leading up to the event, normal routines were disrupted for rehearsals and run-throughs: the whole school got involved. Principal Montoya wanted a block party to showcase the accomplishments of his students and teachers and to give the community a chance to celebrate.

As was the case for IT work related to tablet computers, the ceremony's production, execution, and cleanup depended heavily on student labor. Regular instruction was canceled for several days of rehearsals; a rented stage went up in the courtyard. The day of the event, student ushers greeted visitors at the security gate with a practiced salutation and walked each guest to an assigned folding chair. The program included speeches by visiting state and city government officers, an a cappella singing group, a presentation of the flag by the Cadets (a training organization for students who planned to go directly into the military after high school), the National Anthem, the Black National Anthem, and the Pledge of Allegiance, first in English, then in Spanish. Vice Principal Tustin served as master of ceremonies, introducing each part of the program first in English, then in Spanish. The mother of a current student, a frequent volunteer at the school, took the stage near the start of the speeches. In halting English peppered with Spanish words, Miss Guerrero described how grateful she was for the caring teachers that kept her son safe from gangs and would help him get safely to college. At one point, she called for her son Hector, to point him out to the audience. She scanned the crowd for him, but because the courtyard was crowded, seats jammed in to make room for all the guests and students, she could not see him from the stage. She interrupted her speech for a long moment, searching the crowd, and cried, "Where are you, Hector? I can't see you." That plaintive cry, the mother calling out to her child, evoked laughter from the sympathetic audience. Finally, at the end of the courtyard, near the dumpsters and the fence where feral kittens played, a junior (green polo shirt) stood up, stoop-shouldered and blushing, simultaneously proud of and embarrassed for the attention. "*Mi hijo*," Miss Guerrero said, her voice cracking with affection. "My son," she translated helpfully. The audience applauded riotously for them both.

Next came Mr. Stevenson, member of Academy Schools' Board of Directors, a middle-aged white man in a dress shirt with the sleeves rolled up. He specifically invoked nearby Washington High School, operated by the Los Angeles Unified School District, as a "failed school," one that could not offer the same quality education that Academy schools offered. As proof of their altruism, he reminded the audience that every single member of the Board of Directors of Academy Schools could afford to send their kids to private schools anywhere in the city, but even so had devoted themselves to establishing similar access to quality education for children in South Central. It went without saying that the members of the Board of Directors did not deign to send their children to Academy Charles and Carol Peterson Leadership School, an omission that inspired eyerolls from the teachers in the audience and a few of the parents. He spoke in a monotone inflected with corporate jargon of Academy's effective management team, its successful record of securing federal and foundation grants, its active support for Teach for America, and its "cutting-edge" technological innovations, including the tablet computer program. As if announcing a business forecast, he pledged that Academy schools would continue to expand.

"We should insist that all six hundred thousand students at LAUSD deserve the same education that the kids here at Academy are getting," he said. "We are going to keep at it until every child gets the same education that these kids get." His exit line inspired tepid, polite applause.

July Bertram, founder and CEO of Academy Schools, parent, and former teacher, followed. She welcomed the community to the school and thanked those present for their interest in students. She reminisced on the founding of Academy Schools, how her actions came as a response to dire conditions for students and teachers in LAUSD. This second invocation of the failure of the public school system, a brazenly partisan statement and a rebuke of the work of the LAUSD official seated near her on the dais, did not cause any noticeable discomfort, either in the audience or on stage. All present had heard these talking points many times; aspersions such as these were de rigueur at school functions. She concluded, "Unlike LAUSD, 100 percent of Academy Peterson Leadership School students are accepted to college. We have the same high expectations of all of our students, and we practice accountability." This statistic, merging as it did the past year's matriculation rate with the school's new name, seemed to hover in time, referring simultaneously to the past, present, and future. The number, a sturdy fact that could hold the weight of collective anxiety about the ultimate prospects of the students—the gangs and low expectations and forecasts that haunted earlier speeches—reassured the audience. Ms. Bertram's brief, warm comments also contained an unambiguous evocation of a seemingly indisputable educational value, the "practice" of accountability enabled by data.

After brief and anodyne remarks from a representative of the Los Angeles Unified School District and an envoy of the mayor's office, Principal Montoya, who had served as the school's first and only principal, took the stage to boisterous applause. He described his own experience at the school in starkly emotional terms, a pointed contrast to his customarily fearsome and disciplinarian bearing. He positioned his tenure at the school as a "journey," his voice and body language indicating a charming sincerity: he was nervous, unused to public speaking in front of adults. He related the experience of founding the school in 2007 and recognized some honored graduates and parents in the audience. Voice quavering, he expressed his pride at the courage of his students in resisting a public education system that had failed them and placed this conflict firmly within what he called "a fight for social justice":

> Here we have a really special classroom culture. We are a true educational environment, the kind where students can really learn. Most importantly, we practice accountability of ourselves, our teachers, and our community. Accountability is in everything we do. We graduate 100 percent of the kids, and they all go on to attend a two- or four-year school.

The naming ceremony was an occasion for the school to tell stories about itself, a ritual that gave all present a chance to get on the same page, as it were, about the politics, practice, and meaning of school, another example of Sims's (2017) "sanctioned counterpractices." These activities give participants a shared sense of purpose and a way to talk about communal values, but they happen infrequently. Authorities allow and even laud such aberrations because they allow the organization to tout certain values or aspects of organizational culture, but, overall, they differ greatly from the daily grind of school life, the routines that define life in a place like a public high school in South Los Angeles. Principal Montoya (and Academy CEO Bertram) invoked the matriculation rate of students both as an unequivocal indictor of success and as a reminder to all present of Academy's particular vision of education reform. Numbers make for persuasive storytelling (Dourish & Gómez Cruz, 2018). Indeed, the matriculation statistic continually invoked by Academy leadership to parents like Miss Guerrero told them a story about their child's prospects. According to this story, every child could get into college if the student enrolled at Academy Charles and Carol Peterson Leadership School (or any of Academy's other schools) and if the family followed the school's way of doing things, particularly its tech-focused curriculum. For parents in the neighborhood, many of whom were precariously employed, lacked formal education, or aspired to lift their children into the middle class, this story was a promise that they were not in any position to question. Buttressed by the seemingly irrefutable power of numbers, this promise functioned as both a legitimating principle and a foolproof selling point. Peterson Leadership School/Number Seven's pedagogical and ethical raison d'être rested entirely on the assumption of the failure of public schools and a multivalent appeal to accountability as a solution to this failure. In this story, urban schools have failed to "practice" accountability and, in absolute contrast, Peterson Leadership School/Number Seven (or any of its sister schools) could perform accountability because of their superior values and their superior technological know-how.

Accountability and its attendant practices formed a central object deployed in this assiduously deracialized tale about urban schools, all of which were failing, all of which were racially segregated, and all of which were in poorer neighborhoods.

Accountability, what it means and how to do it, serves as an entry point here into scholarly conversations that have approached the practices of accountability from a broader, sociological perspective: that of surveillance. Accountability, as Principal Montoya described the school's philosophy, is doubly articulated. First, as an ethos of individual responsibility, accountability holds that every person involved in a student's education (e.g., the student, teachers, administrators, parents, or community members) must make needed contributions and, critically, that such contributions *will be captured as data*. Data serves as proxy for these contributions, as purely objective quantifications of any relevant educational event or demographic feature. Second, accountability refers to whatever practices unfold to verify these contributions of students, teachers, and parents, to whatever regime of surveillance is used to assure desired behaviors. This includes any mode of data collection that tracks accomplishment of specific educational outcomes or general norms of behavior. Accountability, either in the form of data capture or in the form of the practices of surveillance that act on such data, presumes a fantastically meritocratic universe: individual students, regardless of their position in society, life experience, personal attributes, or educational history, are made responsible for their own sorting in an outcomes-based hierarchy, one forcefully shaped by documented contributors to academic achievement such as institutional racism, family wealth, place of residence, and other aspects of social class (Lack, 2009; Mijs, 2016).

Storytelling about the needs of poorer students for accountability sets conditions in day-to-day life for the capture, aggregation, manipulation, and analysis of data. The practices to which Principal Montoya, July Bertram, the representative of the Board of Directors, and Miss Guerrero all referred concern the production or consultation of data, captured throughout the school in a wild variety of forms. In a school culture that asserts a strong sense of order over educational techniques and personal behavior, the invocation of data is not merely a common activity, it is a constant of everyday life. Love of children, fear of the future, the precarity of economic life in working-class communities of color, philosophies about learning, the economic interests of educational publishers and technology manufacturers: all these powerful forces find expression in data, much of it captured by the new tablet computers assigned to each student and teacher.

Accountability is a capacious virtue, one to which any number of different, sometimes conflictual programs, policies, routines, or one-off actions can be attributed. These multiple routines all drawn together by the term *accountability* provide a further refinement of the concept of datalogical enframing. While parents, teachers, students, and interested scholars and journalists frequently question the means and ends of student and teacher accountability, the issue is not whether accountability leads to more effective teaching or better outcomes for students: it does not. A significant body of research shows that accountability-based school reforms "have disproportionately disadvantaged urban communities, schools, and children growing up in these communities" (Fisher-Ari et al., 2016, p. 11). What is at issue here is that the accountability story is *productive*. It animates a number of disparate activities and reconfigures resources. It confers benefits to organizations, occasionally to individual students, and never to their communities. Datalogical enframing, then, is a strategy that uses accountability stories as justification, a way for an organization to convince itself that its busyness with data is a kind of tough love that saves students in need from a dangerous fate. Such busyness necessarily produces an alibi for the racialized distribution of access to quality public education, a racial project in which Academy Schools participates and to which it owes its existence.

From Surveillance Schools to Dataveillance Schools

Surveillance studies research has long been interested in schools and their increasing reliance on techniques to sort, monitor, track, control, reward, and coerce subjects, including students, teachers, administrators, and even parents (Monahan, 2011). In school settings, surveillance regimes take many analog and digital forms, combining means to observe physical bodies with emergent modes of "watching, monitoring, tracking, or data analyzing for purposes of control" (Monahan & Torres, 2010, p. 6). Pressure on public schools to demonstrate particular educational outcomes, to produce desired behaviors in students, to teach digital literacy, and to punish student misbehavior in the classroom and elsewhere have resulted in the increased prevalence of surveillance regimes, including school-based police units, closed-circuit cameras, metal detectors, physical inspections of students and devices, zero-tolerance policies, and various forms of data collection and analysis (Gilliom & Monahan, 2012). At the same time, logics of managerial efficiency and personal accountability have transformed the delivery of public education in the English-speaking world over the last two decades, largely through emphasis on data collection, increased use of standardized testing, and the ongoing de-skilling of the teaching profession (Ambrosio, 2013; Apple, 1995; Cochran-Smith et al., 2013; Stassen, 2012). Scholars, teachers, civil society groups, and students themselves have frequently decried the many forms of surveillance that accompany contemporary schooling as invasive and incommensurable with the civic ideals of public education, a phenomenon that chapter 5 will examine in greater detail (Knox et al., 2019).

Surveillance contributes to a carceral educational culture, especially in those minoritized communities where youth are frequently presumed to be dangerous, at-risk, or undisciplined (Raible & Irizarry, 2010; Simmons, 2017). Exclusionary forms of school discipline force students out of school as punishment; these forms of discipline "are concentrated in elementary, middle, and high schools attended by non-White and/or poorer students" (Kupchik & Ward, 2014, p. 332). In this way, urban schools like Peterson Leadership School/Number Seven, created through residential segregation and sustained economic disinvestment, contribute directly to racialized mass incarceration by pushing students out of schools and pulling them into carceral institutions. This action is aided at every step by surveillance regimes and a steady escalation of punishments over minor (or even manufactured) disciplinary infractions (Fine et al., 2003; D. M. Sojoyner, 2016).

Surveillance regimes most often function through multiple, overlapping channels. As Haggerty and Ericson (2000) famously note in their seminal work on surveillance studies, surveillance occurs through multiple modalities and across different scales of time and space. They use the term *surveillant assemblage* to point to the extreme heterogeneity of surveillance techniques, their opportunistic incorporation of all available means of making targets visible via traces of their presence or actions. The authors caution that although research tends to emphasize this or that technological novelty, surveillance is a synthetic game animated by the insatiable desire to look, know, and control, the drawing together of all manner of tools and practices into a distributed gaze. In this way, the capacity for surveillance is infinite, not made of discrete phenomena, but of the continuous desire to expand the surveillant assemblage (p. 610). In addition to this focus on affect as a unifying force in the surveillant assemblage, surveillance research has also attended to the banality of surveillance, the way it operates through everyday technologies, captures daily routines, and becomes a part of the background of lived experience. While fictional accounts of surveillance in film and television focus on glossy, futuristic technologies, real-life surveillance, especially as it is practiced in public schools, has a slap-dash, improvisational character (Monahan, 2008).

Whatever its character, surveillance is a risky business for members of groups differentially targeted by surveillant assemblages, especially for subjects racialized as non-white. Despite its centrality to the practices and consequences of surveillance, scholars have largely siloed racialization and the study of surveillance in schools (and in the surveillance studies literature more broadly). As Simone Browne writes in *Dark Matters: On the Surveillance of Blackness* (2015), academic studies of surveillance have rarely addressed the racialized contours of contemporary surveillant assemblages and the historical influence of legalized programs of control, tracking, and enslavement to which Black people and other people of color have been subjected. Browne argues authoritatively that surveillance is vital to the understanding of the lived experience of Blackness (and vice versa). Browne builds up an archive of art projects, news headlines, technical literature, historical records, and advertising images to reread Haggerty and Ericson's definition of surveillance through the lens of Blackness, in the process prefiguring a number of works related to gendered and racialized norms at work in the optimization of facial recognition and other technologies for lighter-skinned, male features (Buolamwini & Gebru, 2018). Far from being an obscure or rare experience, *racializing surveillance* shapes the very conditions of public life, introducing harsh strictures about who may exist in public and how they may do so. Finally, as Browne notes, an interest in surveillance and the way it shapes and is shaped by race requires a corresponding concern with other forms of "interlocking," socially consequential difference, including class, gender, and sexuality (p. 17).

In the last five years, research on surveillance in schools has specifically taken up those expansions to the surveillant assemblage made possible by datafication, both in the form of technological change and of ideological commitments about the representational capacities of data (Cope & Kalantzis, 2016). To its boosters (frequently commercial entities that sell commercial edtech) and to many of its public detractors, datafied surveillance presumes a mimetic relationship between the digital data that circulates in various administrative circuits and the people and activities so described: in this way, dataveillance, the capture and manipulation of data to sort people or drive behavior is another mode of surveillance, an intensification and acceleration of older, analog methods. The term *dataveillance schools* emphasizes the novelty and prominence of data capture, analysis, and aggregation, frequently through automated analysis and visualization. For scholar of education and digital technologies Ben Williamson, the appeal of such a transformation to schooling has to do with calculability, a guiding but frequently unstated instrumental value at work in the adoption of data-intensive computing in schools. Calculability permits a mode of governance, where the use of commercial technologies by the state (in the guise of public schools) allows it to know, shape, and control its subjects (Williamson, 2017). This form of state management derives its legitimacy from a set of frequently disproven but popularly held assumptions about data, the way that seemingly objective quantitative facts come to stand in for (and replace) a more complex social reality.

Urban schools, such as those operated by Academy Schools, can be an important site of research on dataveillance schools (Jarke & Breiter, 2019). Research has established the significance of school discipline, standardized testing, and technological intervention in the constitution of urban schools, noting in particular how data-intensive technologies demand resources of already underresourced institutions (Crooks, 2019; Taylor, 2013). Such schools face pressure to assure students access to data-producing digital technologies to promote social and economic mobility—the "fight for social justice" invoked by Principal Montoya in his comments at the school's renaming ceremony—but these interventions rarely address the expanded dataveillance risks that these technologies entail (Warschauer & Matuchniak, 2010; Winston, 2007). When families struggle with the consequences of racism and structural poverty, parents and community members will likely have reduced capacity to address surveillance abuse or to advocate meaningfully for responsible use of data captured by educational computing (Boutte & Johnson Jr., 2013; Means, 2013), although, as I show in chapter 5, some communities have organized effective opposition.

My interest in dataveillance schools is rather particular. Despite depictions of dataveillance in popular culture and in certain academic work as absolute, predictive, and inescapable, surveillance as it was practiced in Academy schools was haphazard, post hoc, and unreliable. Despite the way they are presented in influential cultural products like cop shows—as instantaneous, sleek, automated systems that provide the analyst and the detective a perfect, time-stamped replica of the recent past—school-based surveillance regimes tend to be low-fidelity, depending as much on established hierarchies of authority as they do on cutting-edge technology (Alim et al., 2017; Nemorin, 2017). At the level of the school, leadership certainly moved to incorporate new sources of data into their activities, but in practice, they frequently used data to manufacture evidence to justify decisions they had already made. But that reality, counterintuitive as it might be, does not prevent an organization from benefiting from its use of data. Quite the contrary, from the analytic of datalogical enframing, this misunderstanding about the power, vision, and acuity of dataveillance regimes provides a unique opportunity for reputational benefits: couching their activities in terms of data and data-drivenness can make organizations appear sophisticated, capable, and in control.

"I Can Target Exactly Where They Are": Teacher Evaluation

At the end of the 2014–2015 school year, administrators announced that they would institute a long-sought-after policy to establish merit-based pay for teachers. Although administrators presented the plan as novel, some teachers claimed that leadership had been trying to put together such a policy for years and saw the school's technology program as an opportunity to get what they wanted. Charter school advocates have frequently called for merit-based pay structures as part of their market-centric approach. To its proponents, merit-based pay challenges the perceived intransigence of teachers and their unions to education reform, protects talented new teachers from termination due to lack of seniority, and rewards teachers for the success of their students (Brooks, 2020). Merit-pay plans have a long history in education reform, although their ability to increase the quality of public education remains disputed (Murnane & Cohen, 1986). While generalizable benefits of merit-based pay plans have not been established, evidence exists that paying teachers bonuses for improvements in specific outcomes produces a statistically significant increase in those outcomes, but *only* in those particular outcomes (Pham et al., 2021). Although they can be instituted in many forms, merit-pay plans generally include salary bonuses for "high-performing" teachers (i.e., teachers whose students score highly on some specified measurement of learning or accomplishment). Merit-based pay structures can also be formulated to fine or punish low-performing teachers. Unions such as United Teachers Los Angeles have frequently resisted merit-based pay plans in California's public schools, preferring instead evaluation metrics that focus on quality of instruction and pay structures that reward length of service; these issues contributed to UTLA's thirty-thousand-worker-strong strike in 2018 (Stokes, 2018). About half of the charter schools in the United States use some kind of merit-based pay structure (Brooks, 2020).

Academy Schools' technology curriculum did not originally include language about any merit-based pay plan, but the feasibility of such a plan directly linked to the school's efforts in that area. The tablet computer program gave school administrators a number of handy data sources to implement a merit-pay program, one that Principal Montoya and Academy Schools' personnel planned, announced, executed, and revised over a period of roughly six months. The merit-pay plan accorded with Academy Schools' emphasis on accountability, applied here to their own professional staff: by this reasoning, teachers themselves were accountable for contributing to student learning as measured by standardized test scores and other kinds of data, much of it captured from student tablets. In practice, the merit-pay plan depended on the availability of devices to administer tests. While the teachers I worked with most frequently did not openly dispute the plan, many of them candidly expressed reservations about using their students' grades and test scores as markers of the quality of their teaching. After all, many of the students served by Academy had experienced individual life circumstances that would make academic success very difficult, including students who faced extreme poverty, lack of citizenship status, and other kinds of bureaucratic or institutional violence, not to mention many kinds of personal and familial challenges. Teachers also knew that, in general, Peterson Leadership School students would not compare favorably to students from more affluent school districts on nearly any commonly used metric of student achievement (e.g., standardized test scores, grade point averages, completion of AP courses). For all the talk of accountability, teachers privately acknowledged that there were structural, systemic reasons that the "failure" of urban schools could not be addressed by school culture, data-driven or not.

School administrators, prompted by district leadership, embraced this unforeseen benefit of the tablet computer program. More tablets meant more standardized testing. Regardless of its advisability or educational utility, standardized testing itself has become the dominant form of surveillance in schools (Gilliom, 2010; Vinson & Ross, 2000). The presumptive objectivity of data holds that the results of standardized testing produce a value-free measurement of some aspect of learning, "a fair and accurate measurement of individual effort," which in turn allows authorities to sort, rank, discipline, or reward based on data (Au, 2016, 40). Although individual teachers expressed qualms about testing, they had no meaningful opportunity to refuse. School administrators packed the calendar with tests. With more screens, they could test a greater number of students for a longer period of time, in the process meeting a number of state- and district-mandated testing goals. This emphasis on testing was not merely opportunistic, it was purposeful: standardized testing was as central to Academy's particular brand of charter reform as their technology program, another attribute of its pedagogy promoted to differentiate itself from its competitors. Academy Schools took standardized testing seriously, touting on its website, for example, the organization's ability to get higher student scores on tests relative to both the state average and the average of rival school systems. Tablet computers made testing easier for administrators: thanks to the one-to-one program, teachers had enough screens to administer tests to every student in the entire school simultaneously.

In May 2015, administrators canceled all regular classes and dedicated the entire month to a battery of standardized tests delivered via the new tablets. These included state-mandated exams as well as a number of non-mandated assessments specific to Academy Schools. The proliferation of standardized testing in schools is a topic of contentious debate in education research and public policy. Successive presidential administrations—via the Bush-era No Child Left Behind Act and the Obama-era Race to the Top initiative—supported expansion of standardized testing via national requirements and funding incentives, but researchers have frequently pointed to inequitable results of reliance on high-stakes tests and persistent patterns of racial favoritism in their design and evaluation (Au, 2021). Other local schools got in on the testing: Academy Schools had arrangements with for-profit online schools to proctor required tests for their students as well. During the month of standardized testing, the school was fuller than at any other time of year. The state Board of Education required California Standards Tests (CSTs) to measure grade-specific competence in various subjects, including math, science, language arts, and social studies. Seniors also took the annual California High School Exit Exam (CAHSEE), required for high school graduation until 2015. Some students took a battery of tests associated with the Common Core Curriculum that had newly been incorporated into their schools. The Smarter Balanced testing system, specifically designed for delivery via computer screen, featured a number of summative, standards-aligned assessments for juniors that tested performance in math and language arts.

At the end of the school year, as she prepared her classroom for summer school, Ms. Saba, a language arts teacher who had originally been enthusiastic about the tablet computer program, told me that she and the students needed a break from tablets altogether, that overuse of screens had burned them out. Once the month of testing ended, she'd stopped using tablets in instruction all together and instead taken her classes out to the courtyard daily to read paperback copies of *Romeo and Juliet*. She said they all needed some time away from screens "just to recover."

And while Academy Schools certainly had a pedagogical interest in expanding standardized testing, the results of the tests could do double duty. New sources of digital data would finally provide administrators with incontrovertible evidence of teacher quality in a form that the administration could use to reward (or punish) its teachers. Mr. Tustin, the school's third-in-command, a language arts teacher and self-described sports fanatic, was tasked with analyzing various sources of data to come up with metrics of teacher quality. Considered by his fellow teachers to be a masterful user of technology, Mr. Tustin frequently developed workarounds for teachers to use in incorporating tablets in instruction. He also analyzed baseball statistics for fun. Like all three of the school's vice principals, Mr. Tustin carried a walkie-talkie and used it frequently when dealing with disciplinary situations as they flared up over the day: fights, substitutes for sick teachers, bus pickups for away games, the occasionally misplaced tablet computer. He had the air of being in two places at once, his attention always divided between his field of vision and whatever action was being described on the other end of his radio. The same day I spoke with Ms. Saba about her feelings of burnout, a few days after graduation, I came upon Mr. Tustin in his office, setting up a second monitor for his desk. With students off for a few weeks until summer school started, Mr. Tustin had devoted himself full-time to analyzing data related to teacher performance and making final recommendations for individual instructors' evaluations. He was proud to show me his work in this area, excited to geek out with someone else with an interest in data. Without the constant distraction of his radio, he seemed focused, almost meditative. He described his use of data captured from the school's digital technologies this way:

> Being able to use tablets and being able to use technology helps us gather the data faster and easier. . . . I can generate a spreadsheet with all of their [students] scores, I can plug in functions that tell

me how much each student has grown. In the past, to do something like that you're doing it all paper and pencil and you're doing all the math yourself and everything. But, with the use of the technology, we're able to plug numbers in and plug functions in and have it generated immediately for us.

Mr. Tustin's rather ingenious data pipeline collected scores, grades, and other information from all over the school in forms that he could analyze. Data generated from various sources (e.g., commercial platforms, the school's central student information system, teachers' virtual gradebooks) were easily separated from all the things they were taken to represent (e.g., growth, learning, cognition, competence, mastery, scores on a specific assessment) and combined with other kinds of data. Once aggregated, the data then moved through other software environments, ending up as a data visualization. Mr. Tustin described this material transformation of data and how this work allowed him to target low-performing students and their teachers: "I'm looking at the scores school-wide. . . . Once I put it together, I color-code everything. And so I can target that, I can target exactly where they are, and then I can figure out what needs to be done to get them to move up."

Here, the creation of colored targets from data creates a powerful mechanism for directing accountability measures. For students, the consequences of test scores, particularly lower than desired test scores, were immediate. Students were subject to remediation, often in the form of mandatory after-school and weekend "boot camps" aimed at improving scores. Student who failed to attend these after-hours trainings risked expulsion. Likewise, these indicators of success or failure also enabled the new teacher evaluations, in effect allowing data to stand in for two different things.

This reinterpretation of test data, generated via a whole battery of platforms and software environments, greatly differs from the traditional pedagogical interest in assessment in that it relies on decontextualized quantification, lacks any coherent methodology, and has been appropriated by decision-making bodies located far from the classroom (Stassen, 2012). However, test data was not the only kind of data used to evaluate teachers. Ms. Quezada, the math teacher and STL advisor, explained how test data was joined to other kinds of scores in the design of the composite metric that determined teacher rewards or punishments:

> One-third is based on test scores, one-third on parent input, and one-third on your peer evaluation. The community input is fine. Everybody got all the points because the parents didn't really have anything to say. The testing is whatever it is. Then the peer evaluation is really the most important. It's supposed to be weighted the same, but really it's the most important one. That's how [school administrators] treat it.

At the end of June, Mr. Tustin was tasked with telling each teacher what his or her merit-based pay increase would be, or what punishment would be levied should scores require it. During this same period, a number of negotiations of various kinds occurred, including a unionization effort at the school and a number of labor actions related to public schools in Los Angeles. While the promise of performance-based pay in its brute form would mean that teachers would be rewarded or punished based on their composite scores, the actual implementation of the metrics did not accomplish such action. As Ms. Quezada put it, "If they can see you are trying and they like you, you get the maximum raise. I think everyone got the maximum." School administrators determined *retroactively* that all their teachers had performed well and gave this judgment a veneer of quantitative authority.

Despite their technical and logistical success at collecting many kinds of data related to test performance, school administrators balked at using this information to mete out rewards or punishments. This retroactive judgment turned, in part, on that portion of the teacher accountability metric that was supposed to represent community (i.e., parental) input. As scholars in urban education have shown, policies meant to reward parental involvement can inadvertently rely on classist, normative judgments about how to participate in public, assumptions that do not account for conditions in minoritized communities (Boutte & Johnson, 2013; Means, 2013). Although the school had ostensibly instituted the merit-based pay made possible by their expanded data collection powers, every teacher received a significant raise (in many cases, a nearly 30 percent increase in annual compensation) and this increase brought their pay closer to that of their union counterparts in other school districts. The values assigned to each teacher for community input, an empty signifier, tempered the potential influence of the students' highly variable scores on the standardized tests, effectively acting as a buffer.

Between the data collection stage and the eventual implementation of annual raises, school administrators recalibrated what the data was supposed to represent, in effect redrawing the bounds of norm and deviance after the fact. These acts of interpretation became a "politics through which ordinary people can express and mobilize their opposition to surveillance policies" (Gilliom, 2006: 113). In this case, teachers didn't have to do much to resist: they were shielded from any possible negative consequences of the merit pay program by the school administration's retroactive determination that student test scores mattered less than its own professional judgment. On some level, this outcome should throw the whole enterprise of collecting students' testing data to evaluate teacher quality into question. If the administration's professional judgment is more important than other kinds of metrics, why go through the trouble of aggregating data, color-coding targets, and presenting each teacher with a significant raise?

In effect, arguments about what the data could represent, particularly the stand-in for parental opinion, protected teachers from disciplinary measures school administrators devised. However, these contests about data were not themselves understood to challenge the utility of the newly expanded dataveillance apparatus. Leadership ceded the outcome of a particular round of evaluations but affirmed their use of data to shape, sort, and control teaching staff via processes that were opaque at best, arbitrary at worst. In all, a data-driven process largely failed to yield the unambiguous knowledge administrators craved, but the ultimate outcome of this process was not a repudiation of technique, but a valorization of it.

Leadership deployed a strategy or datalogical enframing, a busyness with data that legitimates an organization's approach. This approach to data was productive, in that it conferred a veneer of technical authority, another selling point the school could use to distinguish itself from other public schools. Indeed, every year Academy Schools posts a series of annual reports on its website, including an assessment of each school's efforts. In the case of Peterson/Number Seven, the following year's report boasted of the merit pay system, listing it as one of the distinguishing features of the school. In day-to-day operation, the school administration gained a mechanism to fire or discipline teachers, since the inputs to the end metric of teacher quality were largely based on professional judgment. As Ms. Quezada stated, if leadership liked a teacher, their evaluation would be high. Her statement clearly implied that if leadership did *not* like a given teacher or their performance, they could manufacture evidence of lower performance. In every case, Mr. Tustin's work with data, platforms, spreadsheets, and visualizations gave the administration the evidence it sought. The school's strategy for incorporating test scores and teacher evaluations was deliberately limited: it treated a variety of difficult, complex educational considerations as a straightforward quantitative operation. The work of Mr. Tustin was largely to manufacture an objective equivalent to the expert judgment of school leadership. Locked outside of such quantification would be questions about equity, pedagogy, or labor relations. Again, it would be a mistake to dismiss this strategy as a case of error, naivete, or infatuation with data alone: treating everything as an innocent calculation allowed school leadership tremendous latitude to discipline its at-will employees. Although these creative uses of data were not necessarily dispositive in terms of finding out once and for all which teachers were performing better than others, they were extremely useful, in that leadership's embrace of data gave it legitimacy and reputational benefits. This outcome demonstrates that the organizational strategy of datalogical enframing does not necessarily deliver any kind of insight or actionable knowledge, but, paradoxically, confers legitimacy to the organization, especially its management. In this way, the productive aspects of data-drivenness do not depend on technical or mathematical validity.

On the contrary, almost any kind of analysis can grant an organization the gloss and veneer of mathematical certainty, whether or not the numbers check out.

"Kids Like to Act Stupid": Mandatory College Applications

From the perspective of the school's principal and its three full-time guidance counselors, the incorporation of tablets had been unambiguously successful in student advising (as opposed to the less successful integration in instruction). Access to tablet computers allowed for more college applications to be processed, college applications being perhaps the counseling staff's most important duty from the perspective of leadership. In the 2014–2015 school year, in order to maximize the number of graduating seniors who enrolled in college, the school principal announced a rule that every graduating senior must apply to at least four colleges, using the newly available tablet computers. To manage the application process and its oversight, the school used a commercial platform called Naviance, the use of which has been correlated to an increased college acceptance rate among some student populations (Christian et al., 2017). A failure to apply to the required number of schools (or to apply to more schools should the first four applications be denied) could result in a student being "transferred out" of the school or, in less euphemistic terms, expelled. This aspect of Peterson/Number Seven's discipline was a sensitive subject for school leadership. In their outward-facing promotional material and at important school functions (including prom, graduation, and the renaming ceremony), administrators bragged about Academy's success at getting all of its graduates into college. If students did not cooperate by applying to college, they would threaten this accomplishment.

Led by head counselor Ms. Archer, a deceptively young-looking, thirtysomething Black woman, the three employees in the counseling center served students in all four grades, offering both academic counseling, psychological counseling, and coordination of out-of-school services, including medical and mental health referrals. Ms. Archer, who joked about being mistaken for a high school student at the grocery store and who dressed in flowery, gauzy clothes, maintained a certain emotional contrast to the school's administrators, who tended to project a stern and matter-of-fact attitude. Ms. Archer intentionally managed the counseling center and its nine-computer lab as a peaceful space in the otherwise full and hectic school. Students came to her for help with the most harrowing and difficult experiences of their young lives: violence, pregnancy, drug use, self-harm. The heaviness of these frequent tragedies aside, Ms. Archer's counseling center was perhaps the happiest space in the school, wholly because of her incredible skill in communicating with young people.

Despite her deliberate hands-on approach to counseling ("I'm clueless with computers," she told me), tablet computing changed the shape of her work. Data manipulation and the management of multiple interfaces became part of the work of school counselors. Because of the importance of successful college matriculation to Academy Schools' mission, Principal Montoya depended on Ms. Archer to get all seniors enrolled in a college by the end of the school year. Before the tablet computer program, there had not been enough devices for all the students who needed them: students doing homework or email competed for time with teacher's preparing materials for class, leaving seniors little time on a machine during peak times of the day. Ms. Archer, who liked to read everything in print, maintained one of the only working printers in the building, which made for more traffic in the counseling center computer lab.

To apply to college, seniors created profiles on the Naviance platform. These profiles included many digital files, including required forms (e.g., transcripts, letters of recommendation) and supporting documents (e.g., essays, personal statements, résumés); other forms of descriptive data were imported into these profiles by students, teachers, and counselors (e.g., standardized test scores). Students used their tablets to manage this flow of information, to complete a profile, and to electronically submit this information to college admissions offices. Simultaneously, the Naviance platform generated data about these students in the form of reports, logs, summaries, and dashboards that were accessible to the counselors. In turn, the counselors used dedicated interfaces within the Naviance system to supervise this process, add supporting documents (e.g., admissions fee waivers), count completed applications, identify noncompliant students, and receive notifications of admissions decisions. School counselors used these various sources of data to assemble spreadsheets about student applications, which they then shared with Vice Principal Tustin, who would ostensibly punish noncompliant students.

Several areas of conflict emerged. First, the Naviance platform offered different interfaces depending on a user's status: the counselors saw one "screen" (as counselors referred to these interfaces) on their devices while students saw another. Changes made to student applications could produce changes to the recorded values counselors used to do their work. While this feature allowed counselors to stay current with student activity, it also allowed students reciprocal access to components of the administrative interface, thereby giving students a means to deceive or trick counselors.

Students discovered—sometimes by chance, sometimes through coordinated effort—that they could manually overwrite the outcome of a college application to change their status from rejected to accepted (or vice versa). Students who discovered this hack altered some of their rejections to acceptances for bragging rights, or as Ms. Archer speculated, "just to make themselves feel better." These tactics could frustrate the school's mandatory college applications system, sometimes temporarily, sometimes for long periods of time. As Ganesh (2016) writes, individual strategies of resistance to surveillance regimes are "often manifested in casual, unexpected, ironic, playful, and feeble ways" (p. 168). Ms. Archer and her counselors generally tolerated these feeble efforts so long as students remained compliant in other areas.

Second, some students who wished to evade the monitoring system or its associated punishments could appear to meet their quota of completed college applications by creating and uploading documents filled with gibberish, a strategy of obfuscation. From the administrative interface, a college application would appear complete, but the counselors could not determine that a student had disobeyed unless they were to open and read every individual document for every single profile. In this way, the administrative view was partially obscured. In situations of asymmetrical power, tactics of obfuscation can be effected playfully or mischievously (Bossewitch & Sinnreich, 2013). As another teacher described this familiar tactic, "Kids like to act stupid. If you give them a chance, they'll mess with stuff."

Finally, counselors summarized their work with college applications via a set of spreadsheets they created and shared with school leadership and district administrators. This final transformation could prove difficult because of students' data manipulation:

counselors spent long hours reconciling the contents of their spreadsheets with data in the Naviance system or data held at district headquarters. The ratio of graduating seniors accepted to colleges was used for various administrative purposes, including determining future compensation for the school's principal and counselors. But this ratio was always a rough approximation of some future outcome, a probabilistic reading of who might later enroll in college. As Ms. Archer explained the importance of this metric, "I'm going to do whatever I can to make that number go higher." Her comment invoked the tenuous relationship between the metric derived from various digital objects and the external world. As a practical matter, clearly not all students went on to a two- or four-year college: while the majority of students likely started at some kind of college or university the following fall, some went to the military, some did not enroll, some went to carceral institutions, and some stayed in the neighborhood and did not go anywhere.

For Ms. Archer (and other sympathetic adults), the dataveillance the tablets enabled highlighted a problem with the mandatory applications, one they addressed by tolerating a certain amount of looseness between data and the things that data represented. Poor students, first-generation college students, and students of color face a number of hurdles in completing college degrees (Harmon, 2012). Students of lower socioeconomic status are both less likely to go to college and more likely to leave college without a degree (Zembrodt, 2021). A similar dynamic pertains to racial difference as well: as compared to white and Asian students, Black and Latinx students take longer to complete college, have lower grade point averages, and complete their degrees at lower rates (Martin et al., 2017). These statistics are well-known to Number Seven's staff and faculty. In light of these well-known realities, the school's newly expanded dataveillance regime struck Ms. Archer as misguided. Ms. Archer explained that students might attend the school not out of an endorsement of the school's college application rules but out of desperation:

> We're in an extremely low-income neighborhood. A lot of our kids' family income for the year is maybe $10,000, maybe 15 max, for a family of like four or five. These kids are really, really poor. There's nothing else around here that is a light of hope, and so this school is, for a lot of these families.

Such conspicuous and novel work with data—the decoy documents produced by students, and the spreadsheets and other interfaces managed by a team of counselors whose work demands had suddenly been datafied—were meant to make the frequently invoked statistic of 100 percent college enrollment come true. But no amount of coercion, surveillance, or data work could overcome a more stubborn, naked fact of reality: not all the students wanted or were capable of applying to (much less graduating from) college. As Ms. Archer explained, the work of counseling, at core, was about helping people to help themselves. This duty extended to helping the administration of Peterson/Number Seven feel that they had used every tool at their disposal to create optimal futures for their students, to fulfill the salutary promise of an important number.

There is a great distance between the long hours students spent working on admissions essays, the operations of a vast, cloud-based content management system accessed via tablet computer, the bureaucratic workings of college admissions offices and, finally, a comma-separated values file downloaded from the Naviance system and transformed into a series of spreadsheets. In a sense, the data collected at each step was held as more or less equivalent to every other kind of data. Each data object was functionally conceived of as a link in a chain of representations that reached back to the completion or noncompletion of a college application, which in itself was an object composed of all kinds of digital stuff (Latour, 2013). And while most students played along with this collective agreement, certain students realized, through happenstance or wit, that they could divest one or more of the steps along the chain of data objects of its representational power. In so doing, they could decouple their behavior and the digital traces that stood in for that behavior. The essential dynamic here is that students and some teachers developed means of satisfying the demands of dataveillance while resisting the control these measures sought to effect: they did so by making a strategic show of compliance while exploiting the ambiguity of the representational relationship between digital data and behavior.

Despite the ability of administrators and counselors to capture, view, and analyze data about what students had done or not done with respect to tablet-based college applications, the interpretation of digital data became a narrow space of student resistance. In effect, assumptions about what data represented, clever interventions by students, and tolerance for mischief by school officials allowed some of the subjects of dataveillance to escape coercion. Again, datalogical enframing, an organizational strategy that uses data as an alibi for structural inequality, captures some of the intricacies of the moves and countermoves of dataveillance. Counselors tolerated silly and humorous attempts to escape monitoring as a kind of truce: noncompliant students would not be punished so long as it looked like they were contributing required resources. From the perspective of the organization, its engagements with data (and its purchase of tablets and subscription to Naviance) were productive: they gave the school bragging rights about its total matriculation rate. It also prevented the school from having to acknowledge the deeply unfeasible nature of its 100 percent matriculation rate, its most revered statistic. Busy work with data kept all of these problems contained, orderly, and out of view, but also provided evidence that leadership could use to present itself in the best possible light to its superiors, donors, competitors, and the community at large.

What's So Great about Data?

Given the limitations of data as a way of shaping desired behaviors in teachers and students in the preceding examples, it might stand to reason that school administrators would question the utility of "data-drivenness" so often invoked. After all, school administrators knew which teachers were getting desired results and which ones weren't, just as school counselors largely knew which students had completed college applications and which had not: it was all easy enough to spot in the course of day-to-day teaching. But as I have emphasized throughout this chapter, there is quite a bit of daylight between what data is rumored to be able to do and what it can do in practice. In both examples, school authorities used new sources of data and incorporated some kinds of data analysis into getting people to do what the administration wanted them to do. Even these relatively uncomplicated uses of spreadsheets or dashboards demanded new skills and competence from administrators, staff, teachers, and students. These emerging data routines also inspired clever workarounds or diplomatic hedges: there was a space of strategic interpretation at work, a zone where what meanings data could take on had to be negotiated. Having data did not necessarily give school authorities hoped-for powers and in both cases, resulted in equally innovative forms of resistance in disputes about teachers' labor and students' futures. Data work demanded organizational resources without any corresponding changes in organizational capacity, tactics, or effectiveness.

In terms of the value captured from such activity, these regimes of data collection look very different: for example, Naviance, the company that in 2015 was used by counselors to track college applications, assembled a large corpus of data from the collected works of the many students who—perhaps mandatorily, like the students at Peterson/Number Seven—contributed. Naviance also collected transactional data about its student users and their counselors, adding it to profiles that include creative works such as personal statements, résumés, and letters of recommendation. And while any particular store of data can be difficult to accurately value, the wealth produced by Naviance is quite real. These sources of data form the basis of an asset that has allowed Naviance to change the nature of its business; Naviance, rebranded as an advertising concern, was recently sold by its parent company, the Daily Mail and General Trust. Naviance collects data from students about their interests and proposed careers and degrees; a complementary product, Intersect, sells advertising to colleges and universities. In 2021, these platforms, populated by the free labor of students from all over the world, were sold to a larger edtech company (Power-School) for some $320 million (Wan, 2021).

As Sadowski (2019) writes, data accumulation is itself the point of numerous contemporary enterprises, not only because data can be made to stand in for a variety of things (a score on an exam, a touching personal essay, the amount of time a user stared at her screen before closing a tab), but because data is itself a form of capital, related to economic capital, certainly, but distinct. Contemporary technologies of data accumulation are bound up with cycles of capital accumulation: the commitment that everything in the world can be captured as data is a very lucrative fiction, one that delivers very real fortunes (McKittrick, 2021). Data is its own justification, since the greatest value in data-intensive computation is in creating assets, not necessarily in any particular use or application. That so many supposedly data-driven processes end in a recommendation to collect more data is no coincidence. It should also be noted that whatever value the school itself got from its capture of data, limited as it was, must pale in comparison to the value that Naviance captured from all the schools where it was in use. The community as a whole received no benefit and was positioned merely as a locality from which to extract data.

In effect, the public has become both the site and subject of a story about digital data, a story that correctly understands the increasing value of data, but misapprehends where that value accumulates. In the next chapter, I move out beyond the site of a single school to further sharpen the analytic of datalogical enframing. To do that, I visit an educational organization that serves the very same neighborhoods as Academy Schools, a competitor organization that takes the ethos of data-drivenness even further. In this setting, where tech work, data science, and the entrenched and intractable inequalities of the Los Angeles public schools meet, datalogical enframing provides a way to look at how long-standing and frequently disproven ideas about race get reinscribed in glossy new interfaces.

04 Access as Management

*We refuse to understand data as disembodied and thereby dehumanized
and departicularized. We commit to understanding data as always
and variously attached to bodies; we vow to interrogate the biopolitical
implications of data with a keen eye to gender, race, sexuality, class,
disability, nationality, and other forms of embodied difference.*

CIFOR ET AL., Feminist Data Manifest-no

In the previous chapter, school administrators learned to use newly
purchased hardware to capture data about students and to put
that data to use in surveilling and disciplining students and teachers. Data collection, analysis, and visualization could be incorporated into administrative procedures much more easily than into
classroom instruction. Still, most Academy teaching staff, at least
within the school, generally lacked the technical chops required to
work with data: enterprising people like Mr. Tustin taught themselves how to make use of new sources of data, and importantly,
how to put this data to work via charts, graphs, and other basic visualizations. But there was always something apologetic about how
school staff worked with data, a constant invocation of some kind

of lack of skill or sensibility. Just as teachers frequently confided in me that they didn't use education technology as well or as efficiently as they should, Mr. Tustin told me his data work amounted to "messing around."

I also noted in the previous chapter a pronounced disconnect between data collection and the control of behavior sought via surveillance regimes. As it concerned the power of data to describe and create optimal outcomes, data power was perhaps not all it was cracked up to be. Data did not always confer upon school authorities the ability to achieve desired outcomes because canny subjects of surveillance could find a bit of wiggle room between data and reality and exploit that difference to obstruct, obfuscate, or thwart surveillance. Ironically, this disconnect did not undermine the school administration's ability to enact desired policies (merit pay for teachers and mandatory college applications for students); to the contrary, working with data gave school authorities ammunition to produce justifications for all kinds of things. In my time in the school, I saw teachers use data from tablets to "prove" that students had violated school rules, just as I saw administrators use data to "prove" which teachers produced the best results. A dispute over what a certain source of data meant only affirmed the overall authority of data as a basis for decision-making.

One limitation of my research to this point was that when I asked students, teachers, and administrators where data generated by school computing ended up, I always got the same answer: "I don't know." I became curious about how the larger organizations that manage individual schools were adapting to the greater prevalence of data enabled by access-based policies and the general proliferation of edtech in classrooms. To answer that question, I spent some time working with a team of data specialists employed by another charter management organization, one that serves the very same working-class communities of color in South and East Los Angeles as Academy Schools.

"Promoting a Data-Driven Culture"

CMO-LAX is another not-for-profit charter management organization that operates under the umbrella of a national foundation: the regional organization and the national foundation share resources and data. CMO-LAX operates thirteen middle and primary schools in South and East L.A., representing some ten thousand students. Like Academy Schools, CMO-LAX schools serve minoritized, lower-socioeconomic-status communities exclusively: 99 percent of students identify as Black and/or Latinx and 91 percent of students qualify for free lunch. CMO-LAX's schools are also intensely racially segregated (Orfield & Ee, 2014). Given the growing power and prestige of data in public education, one can read the motto of CMO-LAX as both hopeful and troubling: "Promoting a Data-Driven Culture." Conspicuously, this motto was also once used by the publisher of Tableau, a commercial data visualization platform that figures prominently in the material that follows.

CMO-LAX's official mission—to "teach the academic skills, foster the intellectual habits, and cultivate the character traits needed for our students to thrive in high school, college, and life"—concerns a specific strategy of charter-based education reform. CMO-LAX seeks to achieve the growth of its network by demonstrating superior educational outcomes as compared to traditional public schools in Southern California. CMO-LAX then promotes itself via publications, videos, public presentations, and appeals to various government agencies and private philanthropies. Arguments supported by various forms of data are central to the mission of the network and its demonstration of its own capabilities.

CMO-LAX promotes itself as a data-driven alternative to traditional public schools, as an innovator. In a brochure, CMO-LAX writes, "By measuring what matters and using real-time data to assess student achievement, teachers can maximize the impact of instructional technology on student growth." The same document promises that CMO-LAX will also contribute to the dissemination of best practices. This conspicuous invocation of putatively impartial and depoliticized "data-driven decision-making" functions as a sign of organizational quality, competence, and future-orientation, a selling point in a fraught marketplace of public, private, and quasi-public education that working-class communities of color in Southern California must navigate (Buras & Apple, 2005; Pearman & Swain, 2017).

The banal term *district headquarters* might bring to mind images of Southern California Brutalist architecture and airless interiors jammed with heavy filing cabinets. CMO-LAX headquarters, located on a busy strip next to juice bars, coffee shops, and brunch spots that cater to East LA's newly arrived young professionals, seems chosen specifically to contrast with that dull image. The front doors of the office, two heavy wood double doors that remain from the building's previous incarnation as a garage, lead to a large receptionist's desk, behind which is visible a scrum of youthful workers. The whole ground floor of the office is filled by up to twenty workers. They gather in small groups around a computer monitor for an impromptu collaboration or take calls in a narrow stairwell, wherever they can find a bit of space. Here or there, a twentysomething sits on the floor typing on a laptop in a posture familiar to academic conferences and airports. Up a winding black staircase, the second floor is less crowded, but more conspicuously references some of the spatial and aesthetic touches of the tech sector: a large open plan office of roughly fifteen desks spreads out under a high, vaulted ceiling. Each region of desks and cubbies corresponds to a function of the organization: real estate, marketing, data. The most private and spacious offices, located on a mezzanine level just below the ceiling, are reserved for the organization's chief executives.

Between 2016 and 2018, I observed CMO-LAX's Data Team. At the time of my field work, eight full-time employees and one intern formed the Data Team; the group itself was formed of two sub-teams, each supervised by the director of data and analytics, as illustrated in the following personnel breakdown. (The number in parentheses notes length of tenure at the conclusion of my field work in 2018.) These teams collaborated frequently, but were conceived as dividing data work into input and analysis.

CMO-LAX Data Team

Director of Data and Analytics (8 years)

Analytics Team (analysis)	*Student Information Team (input)*
Chief Data Scientist (5 years)	Senior Student Information Manager (4 years)
Data Scientist (3 years)	Student Data Systems Analyst (5 years)
Data Analyst (1.5 years)	Data and Student Information Associate (4 years)
	Human Resources Systems Analyst (1 year)
	Human Resources Intern (1 year)

The Student Information Team ("SI"), the team tasked largely with the input of data, worked more closely with schools and supervised the configuration and standardization of fields in the organization's centralized student information system (SIS), a form of commercial, web-based database. The Analytics Team ("Analytics"), on the other hand, dealt primarily with aggregating or analyzing data captured from many different sources, typically working on tasks such as creating data pipelines or addressing organization-wide questions assigned to it by executives. Analytics was generally considered more technically sophisticated than SI. Each staff member of the larger Data Team (both Analytics and SI) submitted examples of their work for purposes of my research and agreed to follow-up interviews to comment on the work they had submitted. In addition, I joined the team's monthly all-hands staff meetings and attended professional conferences with team members. Several team members agreed to more extended interviews over a period of six months. I collected examples of code, writing, and data visualization produced by team members. I also hung out with team members in small group activities and social functions such as birthday parties or happy hours.

In a 2017 interview, Ella, Student Data Systems Analyst—a data professional and Latina resident of one of the working-class neighborhoods her organization serves—reflected on what it means for a public-serving organization to enact a data-driven ethos:

The way I conceptualize it is of course you have the data, and the data then gets pushed to the teacher, to the student, to the parent and then that impacts the community, and that's how I see it and I think that's what keeps me at CMO-LAX. . . . I think a lot of the times, I reflect back on my own experience of my parents and them not really going to my parent conferences, or not really understanding what I was doing, or not being able to help me with my homework. How do you translate that into data?

Ella's statement is instructive for a number of reasons. First, it demonstrates a sentiment frequently expressed by CMO-LAX's data professionals with respect to the organization's mission, how care applied to data work functions transitively, and how data "pushed" to students and parents "impacts the community" for the better. Ella's comment also ends with a provocative question about translation via data. She aspires to a kind of data work that could capture the complexity, contingency, and specificity of experience. Ella also links this effort to persistent shortcomings, particularly to resources that families should contribute to educational activities, a common pedagogical commitment of many schools that serve minoritized communities (Dishon & Goodman, 2017). Conspicuously, in all of my interviews, Ella and her colleagues at CMO-LAX frequently reiterated the need for more data to accomplish their organization's mission, this despite the many sources and varieties of data to which they already had access. Interpreting data for a "data-driven" organization almost always meant wrestling with the insufficiency of data.

What I found at CMO-LAX was a way of working through the fundamental ambiguity of data by adopting the tools, techniques, and aesthetics of the tech sector. Despite a heterogeneous set of views about the potential of such work to contribute to the improvement of public education for their exclusively Latinx and Black students, data professionals relied on a single medium to communicate their interpretations of data to other members of the organization, including school personnel. A bespoke platform of 125 dashboards afforded a graphical means of conveying objectivity, certainty, and actuarial foresight, even in cases where data professionals doubted the validity of their own analyses. Data professionals were encouraged to produce visual displays that supported the mission of the organization and its story of racial uplift, and, in this way, racial concepts crept into supposedly objective analysis. Whether the data work touted by this organization produced better education than any other organization was expressly beside the point: datalogical enframing removed any such question from organizational view. This strategy allowed the organization to claim to mitigate racialized outcomes in the "intensely segregated schools" it administered, and, simultaneously, to accommodate the racial project that creates, funds, and maintains such segregated schools (Orfield & Jarvie, 2020).

"All Data Is Problematic"

As Perrotta and Williamson (2018) have argued, the impetus to incorporate data-intensive technologies into schools is powerful, a self-reinforcing loop that positions data analysis as a solution for educational problems and presents education as a series of technical problems. The impulse to be data-driven is a move to shift decision-making into the computational register, to automate and rationalize complex decisions about resources, ethics, and goals via "accelerated knowledge that enables organisations to be increasingly responsive, nimble and reactive to market pressures"(Beer, 2017, p. 22). Data work applied to urban education represents a drastic imposition of market logics into schooling, recasting students not as learners, but as "prized products, from which valuable behaviours can be extracted and consumed by ever-improving algorithmic systems" (Knox et al., 2019, p. 5). As scholars have long maintained, the digital data upon which such analysis depends is never "raw" and must be interpreted by communities of interest (Borgman, 2015; Gitelman, 2013). Algorithms, a topic of intense scholarly interest in techno-social research, stand in synecdochic relation to these communities of interest, to the networks of platforms, software, organizations, people, scripts, code libraries, technical standards, and other entities deployed in pursuit of the oracular power of digital data (Burrell, 2016; Dourish, 2016; Noble, 2018; Seaver, 2017).

As it concerns the rapidly expanding market for data-intensive computing applied to education, those symbolic systems that define racial projects increasingly take the form of digital data, creating a political and representational system where the pursuit of "quantitative objectivity" masks the continuous subordination of racialized groups (Gillborn et al., 2018, p. 158). Education research, practice, and policy in the United States incorporates many quantitative practices that tacitly enshrine the "permanent inadequacy" of minoritized subjects (Butler, 1996, p. 199). As scholars have frequently pointed out, data-intensive modes of decision-making promise objectivity by transforming phenomena into data via processes of representation (Drucker, 2014; Neff et al., 2017). Some respondents' explanations of their own work with data draw into question any thoroughgoing commitment to this representationalist paradigm. Data work at CMO-LAX accommodated a variety of conflicting views about what data is, what it can say, and how it might legitimately be used in public schooling. For data professionals on the Analytics Team especially, questioning the representational power of data was part of the job.

Notably, all team members expressed unanimous support for the goals of urban education as practiced by the CMO. They viewed their careers as contributions to the improvement of the minoritized communities the CMO serves: two of the interviewed team members spoke of their work with data as intimately related to the experience of growing up in the same communities served by the CMO. In this way, the politics of the charter school movement form a background against which team members understood their own efforts. Admirably, they viewed their work with data as ameliorative and community focused.

In scientific collaboration, organizational structure has been shown to influence the ways that data is produced and the way that it circulates (Vertesi & Dourish, 2011); a similar dynamic is particularly pronounced at CMO-LAX, even though, in many cases workers use similar data, tools, platforms and software (e.g., Python, SQL, Excel). Although both Analytics and SI worked together closely, their respective approaches to data contrasted greatly.

On the SI team, data was generally taken as an unproblematic proxy for people, places, or events. If team members were concerned about the limits of what data could represent, they expressed this as concern with the extensiveness or quality of data, not as a limit of its representational power. Data was held as distinct from the things it represented, but it stood in mimetic relation to its referents. What's good for data is also good for the students so represented. Any deficiency in representational capacity was error. While team members frequently questioned specific qualities of the data they worked with, its timeliness or its accuracy, they did not dispute its representational status. This resulted in a sort of transference, where working on data meant working on students, which also meant working to improve communities.

Both the data scientist and the data analyst held other positions previously at CMO-LAX and were promoted for gaining new technical skills. In terms of experience, all three members of Analytics learned vital programming skills on the job, often on the SI Team. As the Analytics manager explained, "You have to be able to do the work, but we value more being passionate about education." In this sense, programming skills were less important than an understanding of CMO-LAX's mission. If the work of data analytics involves a particular approach to problem solving, a way of balancing abstraction and interpretation, these interviews suggest that, at least at CMO-LAX, such "professional vision" would also have to be complimented with considerable specific knowledge of public education and charter reform (Passi & Jackson, 2017; Schutt & O'Neil, 2013).

Here, the data scientist summed up the team's approach:

A lot of what I do is trying something out, seeing if it "looks right," double checking it, modifying something small, then rerunning it to try it again until I know that it's correct. Once it's in Tableau, it can be harder to detect issues because there's often a lot more aggregation or calculation going on that can obscure a faulty data point, so you have to be extra vigilant about what you're doing.

In further interviews, all members of Analytics expressed similar concerns about making sure their outputs were "reasonable," or that results were "in scope." As the Analytics manager put it, "All data is problematic." This playful comment referred to the fundamental ambiguity of data work, the way that manipulating stores of data could yield results that no longer referred to anything out in the world. Work on Analytics frequently required a reflexive component, a way of working "until I know that it's correct." A certain amount of "messiness" was assumed here, a presumption of the occasional "faulty data point." This comment also indicates a shift to a different interpretive strategy: the creation of graphical analytics in the commercial software platform Tableau. As this respondent made clear, Tableau might mask uncertainty, presenting as settled what might be an unresolved question.

Data Team members produced dashboards that presented data as trustworthy and definitive, not because they had necessarily made such a determination, but because the visual organization of information carried those associations. As Drucker (2014) argues, it is precisely an overfamiliarity with these modes of representation that make them so persuasive. As a corrective, she calls for a theory of humanistic visual knowledge (*graphesis*), a way of valorizing forms of looking and seeing that are separate from the logocentric and statistical worlds of science and business. For now, it is sufficient to point out that the use of dashboards tends to point toward particular kinds of reasoning and particular kinds of conclusions in what pretends to be an objective, mathematical description. Just as physical spaces support some kinds of behavior and deter others, visual displays and interfaces support or impede certain kinds of thinking (Farman, 2012; Few, 2006; Schüll, 2014).

Making Real-Time Truants

Data work at CMO-LAX involved capturing data about students and their families, but only in those forms that satisfied preexisting normative commitments about data-drivenness and about the relationship between individual behavior and educational outcomes. Specifically, the "real-time data" that CMO-LAX's promotional materials touted became real only when converted to some format that could be hosted on a commercial platform and thereby abstracted from the racialized subjects it described. The Data Team's analysis and visualization looked for patterns in data that would shape organizational or pedagogical behavior, but it did so not by any special acuity or analysis, but by transforming traditional sources and types of data into newer formats.

In a 2017 interview, CMO-LAX's chief student information officer, Nina, explained that what the organization really needed to fulfill its mandate to become data-driven was data about behavior. As the highest-ranking permanent staff member of SI, Nina dealt largely with standardizing procedures and data fields to record student-level information. California's public K–8 schools must report many forms of student-level data to regional, state, and national authorities: such reporting has been a feature of public education for decades and many efforts at establishing national education standards over the past thirty years dictate requirements for reporting (Egalite et al., 2017; Holbein & Ladd, 2017). Nina imagined a way of collecting needed data without the active intervention of her and her team:

> My goal would be to have the flow of student information happening very naturally and for all of that to be like a well-oiled machine, so that as many people as possible can focus on kids. . . . I want collection to be part of the everyday process, where it's just super clean and smooth.

Nina indicated that the Data Team's work was extensive and demanding: where the value of such labor accumulated was not stated, but according to Nina's interview, these resource demands might possibly have stood in the way of "focus on kids."

At the time of the interview excerpted above, Nina had just completed a project focused on identifying chronically absent students. Researchers argue that the causes of chronic absenteeism are complex, but include factors such as environmental, familial, and individual characteristics, as well as school type (e.g., charter vs traditional) (Lenhoff & Pogodzinski, 2018). However chronic truants came to be and whatever reasons accounted for this status were not of interest to Nina's project. Getting data about chronic truants stored in the correct form on the correct platform was the focus. This task proved technically difficult and intellectually challenging because, as Nina explained it, finding out which students had missed enough school to be considered chronic truants "involved a lot of trial and error, and some guesswork":

> My initial results were not matching what I knew about student attendance rates at our schools. Specifically, my report was reflecting chronic absentee rates that were lower than what I knew them to be. In order to get the correct figure, I had to take raw data (i.e., students' attendance records per each date of enrollment), filter out anything other than "presents," and pull in the number of days each student was enrolled over the course of the year. While this seems simple, attendance data is very nuanced in our student information system, so the process to get it right was slow and painstaking at times. Fortunately, our team has been able to create a dynamic dashboard in our data hub that reflects chronic absentee rates at any given day.

Nina's evaluation of the process she had ("slow and painstaking"), as opposed to the kind she wanted ("super clean and smooth"), corresponded to a distinction visible in the interface as

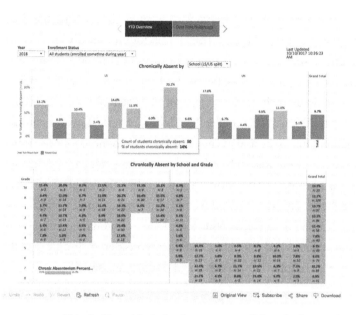

FIGURE 5. This dashboard includes the measures of chronic absenteeism. Presumably, Gia's code would lead to a similar dashboard in the data hub. Image by author.

a division between dashboards that summarized "enrollment" and those that related to "attrition/behavior" (see Figure 5). Expressly, Nina's work involved eliminating ambiguity in data, reformatting, recounting, and recalculating to eliminate undesirable nuance.

Nina's supervisory position gave her professional responsibility for the ongoing collection of extensive demographic descriptions of all of CMO-LAX's current and former students, including age, race, address, place of birth, and citizenship. Likewise, her student information system contained extensive information about students' families: the size, number, and marital status of household members, the education level of parents/guardians, annual family income, and so forth. In short, Nina's take on the utility of different forms of data, repeated frequently in my interviews with other member of the organization, was that the data they had took the wrong shape, that it did not track the right things, and that it did not lend itself to explaining the kinds of things they wanted to know (Kelly, 2017). In the case of nearly all my work with CMO-LAX's data, one aspect was routinely shunted out of view: the race of the people described by the CMO's database, 98 percent of whom were Black or Latinx. In this way, data work at CMO-LAX devalued descriptions of race in their analyses (data that was "just demographic"), but attributed explanatory power exclusively to data that stood in for individual behavior. In short, data aggregation, analysis, and visualization produced and framed a completely deracinated explanation for the figure of the "chronic truants" that this work was creating, partly through "painstaking labor" and "guess work."

Of note here is that Nina's difficulties did not concern whether or not schools had taken attendance and reported correctly: the issue concerned the ability of the Data Team to incorporate such banal and frequently analog modes of data collection into its "data-driven" apparatus. As Nina described it, she and local school administrators had a general sense of when and where absenteeism was a problem. Nina supervised how school administrators did their reporting, how the fields of CMO-LAX's SIS were configured, and how graduates and their families would be represented in the database ("raw data"). However, this "painstaking" work was merely preparation for something "dynamic."

Later, Nina showed me the fruits of her months-long attempt to make reports of chronic absenteeism useful: a series of dashboards displayed in a data hub available to select members of the organization, including a series that incorporated reports of chronic absenteeism. Nina gave me a tour of this data hub, a set of interactive data dashboards constructed by Nina's counterparts in Analytics. Whitman (2020) described the work of university-based data professionals charged with collecting, aggregating, and analyzing data for the purposes of altering student behavior. Data professionals valued data that described behavior over demographic data, in effect begging the question of how certain forms of individual action might influence desired academic outcomes. At the same time, the author described how those same data professionals understood many aspects of student success to be tied to race, wealth, sex, or gender, characteristics that did not suit the organization's emphasis on individual behavior. This dynamic also obtained in data work at CMO-LAX.

From an organizational perspective, CMO-LAX's datalogical enframing involved altering existing data collection regimes to accommodate newer tools and platforms common to private-sector data science, especially the commercial visualization platform Tableau. Noteworthy here is the presumed audience of the dashboard: CMO-LAX's data hub was only partially viewable by classroom teachers and school principals. At the time of my field work, the Data Team did not consider classroom teachers, parents, or other school-level stakeholders as an audience for data work. This work was used internally to provide managerial overview to the organization's leadership and externally to promote the organization's use of data to other educational organizations and funders. From the analytic of datalogical enframing, CMO-LAX's invocation of data-driven methods served to obscure the racial distribution of resources, including access to racially integrated public education by the subjects captured in its database.

"Real-time data," the goal of CMO-LAX's data work and a point of pride in its marketing materials, reified certain representations (to the exclusion of others) and demanded extensive resources to shape and store data in ways more typical of tech sector entities. In the next section, the representations made real by data work are incorporated into calculative regimes and used, ironically, as the basis to justify further data collection. What is of interest here is not the advisability or inadvisability of charter-based school administration or the veracity of the laudatory claims of marketing departments, but the specific ways that data-drivenness manifests in urban schools and how it operates with respect to racial projects.

Visualizing College Success

The next section concerns a transformation of the data collected by Nina and her direct reports. In what follows, data professionals attempted to incorporate modes of analysis and visualization common to private industry to encourage "college success," or the eventual matriculation of their students at a four-year college or university (an organizational imperative reminiscent of the mandatory college applications in the previous chapter). In doing so, these professionals enacted a strategy of datalogical enframing—searching for some previously unknown pattern in data that might improve student performance and, simultaneously, ignoring well-understood dynamics that constrain the educational opportunities of the minoritized communities they serve. Datalogical enframing does not necessarily deliver any kind of insight or actionable knowledge, but, paradoxically, results in a demand for more data. Any kind of analysis results in a demand for more data.

As chief data scientist at CMO-LAX, Gia was responsible for the most sophisticated and technically demanding forms of data work in the organization. Her work consisted of developing data pipelines, of making the various platforms CMO-LAX and its schools used in all their various tasks and at all their various sites interoperate. Data work done in schools tends to "take the form of simple arithmetic rather than complex algorithms; manual rather than automated calculations; and a reliance on unsophisticated technical and classificatory procedures" (Selwyn, 2016, p. 63). Gia herself did not consider most of her work mathematically or computationally sophisticated. Although she used many tools common to data science work in private enterprise—Python, Amazon Web Services, SQL, and Tableau—she described CMO-LAX's capacities as unsophisticated compared to the kind practiced in tech firms; she felt part of her job was to help the organization catch up to industry. Gia had been working for some months to answer a question: how could CMO-LAX help more of its students complete college? To that end, Gia shared some code she had been developing.

Gia's code sought to predict which of its primary and middle school students (grades K–8) would complete college. Black and Latinx students complete college degrees at lower rates than do members of other racial and ethnic groups, even when socioeconomic status is controlled for (Bowen et al., 2011; Martin et al., 2017). In a description of her efforts in this area, Gia described her motivation like this,

> Our first cohort of eighth graders graduated high school only six years ago, which means we don't have a ton of data on our college students reaching back to middle school. I am looking into

middle school to high school success indicators and then using those high school indicators to determine what factors contribute to matriculation.

Below is a program written in R with Gia's comments. The code tries to predict "college success" based on grades and test scores of junior high school students.

```
> ## regression
> logit1 <- glm(fouryearcollegepersistence ~ highest_sat_crm_score + cum_
gpa.y.whole, family = "binomial", data = final.data.lt.2016)

Call:
glm(formula = fouryearcollegperisistence ~ highest_sat_crm_score + cum_
gpa.y.whole, family = "binomial", data = final.data.lt.2016)

Deviance Residuals:
                Min         1Q      Median        3Q        Max
             -2.1952    -0.7708      0.5101    0.7608      .5289

Coefficients
                        Estimate   Std. Error   z value    Pr(>|z|)
(Intercept)            -6.750486     1.660725    -4.065   4.81e-05***
highest_sat_crm_score   0.003613     0.001059     3.412   0.000644***
cum_gpa.y.whole         0.009535     0.003672     2.597   0.009417**
- - -
Signif. Codes: 0 '***' 0.001 '**' 0.01 '*' 0.05 '.' 0.1 ' ' 1

(Dispersion parameter for binomial family taken to be 1)

Null deviance:       181.111 on 154 degrees of freedom
Residual deviance:   152.87 on 152 degrees of freedom
(578 observations deleted due to missingness)
AIC: 158.87

Number of Fisher Scoring iteration: 5

> create college success index from logit1 model
> final.data$collegesuccess <- 0
> final.data$collegesuccessindex <- -6.750486+0.003613*final.data$highest_sat_
crm_score+0.009535*as.numeric (final.data$cum_gpa.y)
>
```

```
> ## regressions that use MS statistics
> reg4 <- lm(collegesuccessindex ~ + nnwea_rit_Mathematics_8_Fall + days_
absent8, data = final.data)
> summary(reg4)

Call:
lm(collegesuccessindex ~ + nnwea_rit_Mathematics_8_Fall +
days_absent8, data = final.data)

Residuals:
               Min        1Q      Median      3Q       Max
              -1.665     -0.765    -0.101     0.669    2.888

Coefficients
                                Estimate   Std. Error  z value  Pr(>|z|)
(Intercept)                     -5.805172   1.349607   -4.301   3.52e-05***
nnwea_rit_Mathematics_8_Fall     0.015378   0.005963    2.579   0.0111*
days_absent8                    -0.029513   0.021343   -1.383   0.1693
- - -
Signif. Codes: 0 '***' 0.001 '**' 0.01 '*' 0.05 '.' 0.1 ' ' 1

Residual standard error: 0.9318 on 118 degrees of freedom
(2236 observations deleted due to missingness)
Multiple R-squared: 0.06174, Adjusted R-squared: 0.04583
F-statistic: 3.882 on 118 DF, p-value: 0.02329

Code detail:
> ## regression
> logit1 <- glm(fouryearcollegepersistence ~ highest_sat_crm_score + cum_
gpa.y.whole, family = "binomial", data = final.data.lt.2016)
```

Gia's code proceeded in roughly four logical steps. First, the code creates a logistic regression model based on two variables. This operation posits college matriculation as a dependent binary variable ("fouryrcollegepersistence"), the value of which is predicted by two independent variables. The CMO's K–8 students are too young to take Scholastic Aptitude Tests (SATs), the most widely used college entrance exam in the United States. However, the chief data scientist has a number of SAT scores of *former* students available to her, recognizable in the code as the variable called "highest_sat_crm_score." The CMO vigorously collects many kinds of information about its graduates, including eventual high school performance, which forms the basis for the variable called "cum_gpa," the cumulative high school grade point average. What results for the first part of this code is a model that demonstrates a strong relationship between GPA, SAT scores, and college persistence. As academic research has generally shown, higher GPAs and higher SAT scores correlate with measures of college persistence: students who perform well on these indicators in high school frequently complete undergraduate degrees (Wolfe & Johnson, 1995). Here, trusted statistical techniques have confirmed this observed tendency and, quite usefully, given some sense of how strong the relationship is between the variables of interest for a small set of observed values.

The next step in the program uses the model generated by the logistic regression to predict college persistence for the *entire* population of students described in the data by GPA and SAT score, not just those for the subset of students for whom such data has been collected.

```
Code detail:
> create college success index from logit1 model
> final.data$collegesuccess <- 0
> final.data$collegesuccessindex <- -6.750486+0.003613*final.data$highest_sat_
crm_score+0.009535*as.numeric (final.data$cum_gpa.y)
```

For the many students about whom she has incomplete data, the data scientist makes an inductive leap, assuming that the model she has created will apply to all of her students and not just those about whom she has been able to access empirically observed data.

The last operation of the code performs another regression, this time a linear regression.

```
Code detail:
> ## regressions that use MS statistics
> reg4 <- lm(collegesuccessindex ~ + nnwea_rit_Mathematics_8_Fall + days_
absent8, data = final.data)
> summary(reg4)
```

This regression seeks to arrive at the same distinction made by "college success index," but to arrive at that target based on two *different* independent variables: one a score on a standardized test given to eighth graders ("nwea_writ_Mathematics_8_Fall") and the other a measure of absenteeism ("days_absent8"). This is exactly the same measure developed by Nina in the previous section of this chapter.

The final operation checks the validity of the model. In this case, the relationship established is weak: junior high school metrics do not strongly predict college persistence. The data scientist described her own evaluation of the code: "I'm finding that a lot of the predictive power gets lost this way."

Regardless, the chief data scientist decided to implement this analytic provisionally. Lacking any better model to describe the relationship between junior high school metrics and eventual matriculation, the chief data scientist planned to share her analysis and also resolved to collect more data to improve and validate her work. While the desired relationships between variables sought did not emerge, the chief data scientist reasoned that this work, even if imperfect or not especially reliable, could prove more useful to administrators than the alternative, which would be to have no data at all. Her move to share this work also serves to overstate the relationship between data and behavior, even though, by her own careful calculations, no such relationship could be strongly determined. This bespoke analytic, so particular to the environment where it was written and sensitive to the vagaries of the data upon which it operated, provides a concrete way to understand datalogical enframing: from an organizational perspective, data-drivenness appears not just as a technique for directing activity, but as an organizational goal in and of itself. Tested statistical techniques, deep domain knowledge, and entirely novel and selective procedures mingle here, but instead of providing unambiguous or decisive evidence for one course of action or another, they reinforce a demand for more data. Organizations invested in "numeric authority and continuous growth" use numbers in ritualistic or emotional ways to direct employee behavior, but at CMO-LAX, it is not a final output or target that is of consequence, but the Data Team's calculative capacity (Mazmanian & Beckman, 2018, p. 375). This voraciousness with respect to data assures both the organizational necessity of the Data Team and the value proposition of CMO-LAX in the education sector.

Like any competent, reflexive practitioner, the chief data scientist was intensely aware of the limits of data analysis, particularly as it concerned the predictive power of models: as part of her professional skill set, she had terms available to measure and describe the error of the model she had created and was perfectly up-front about these limits. After the publication of the dashboard in the data hub, these terms were locked out of analysis, obscured beneath the orderly planes of a data visualization that did not register uncertainty, error, or ambivalence. Organizationally, what the data said was of less importance to CMO-LAX's data-drivenness than the presence of the dashboard itself. In the end, the demand for data was always open-ended: the Data Team always advocated for more data, effectively guaranteeing their own authority and centrality to the organization's mission. In this way, data-drivenness confers status both inside and outside the organization.

Data-Driven for What?

At CMO-LAX, datalogical enframing accompanied and occluded the use of deficit-informed analyses (Davis & Museus, 2019; Sharma, 2018) and updated them for industry-standard tools and platforms. Throughout my fieldwork, data did not offer clear directions or unambiguous answers, although these patterns were frequently assumed to be present despite a lack of evidence. The most frequent answer to any sustained process of analysis was a request for more data. In this way, data work became not just a means to support organizational decision-making, but an end in and of itself. What data stood in for was largely irrelevant. The work of the Data Team supported CMO-LAX's mission to improve its schools, all of which serve minoritized communities, and to disseminate practices that would improve all such schools. By reimagining itself as an innovative, technologically sophisticated, data-driven organization, CMO-LAX could tout its technological capacities and expand its network of schools. These associations implicitly criticize other public schools as lacking such capabilities and imply that the academic accomplishments of students should be attributed to organizational culture. Datalogical enframing prevents consideration of the racial projects to which the organization contributes and instead produces demands for data.

Again, I am not arguing CMO-LAX (or any of the other urban schools I studied) cause the extreme racial segregation of schools in Southern California. What is significant here is that CMO-LAX *presupposes* racially segregated schools and uses data to confer reputational benefits that have little to do with quantitative analysis and everything to do with capitalizing on the increasing cultural cachet of data, the imagined potential of data-intensive computation to render the world legible, predictable, and manageable. In many ways, this pursuit of reputational benefits overrode any organizational imperative for equity or social responsibility. As Ray (2019) describes this dynamic, organizations contribute to racialization in that they "decouple formal commitments to equity, access, and inclusion from policies and practices that reinforce, or at least do not challenge, existing racial hierarchies.... This decoupling allows organizations to maintain legitimacy and appear neutral or even progressive while doing little to intervene in pervasive patterns of racial inequality" (p. 42).

Datalogical enframing names CMO-LAX's strategy of making the data it had conform to the tools and platforms of data work in the private sector. Datalogical enframing likewise concerned the Data Team's mandate to make its derived analyses and visualizations appear sophisticated for management and select audiences. However it appeared, and whatever tools it used, data work at CMO-LAX deliberately and purposively invoked some association with the tech sector to burnish its own reputation. Datalogical enframing put off harder questions about resources in favor of valorizing the organization's own approach. CMO-LAX claims to be better at schooling via data-drivenness, but its exultation of data does not extend to questions about the conditions that segregate schools and how CMO-LAX's activities might legitimate this racial project. My point is not that there exists some other, perfectible, more agreeable version of datafied public education. To the contrary, my point is that the contradictions, assumptions, and value judgments on display in this field site are productive: they confer benefits to the organization and help it to expand. Data captured in the name of making urban schools work better via technology ends up as a reputational resource for the charter management organization. Select individuals might get a better or worse educational experience, but the value of whatever is captured cannot be redistributed to the community itself: the community doesn't even register in these calculations and exchanges.

Contemporary technologies of data aggregation, visualization, and analysis offer powerful ways to know the world. Technological access (particularly in minoritized and racialized communities) is frequently presented as a strictly value-add proposition: if the technology works as advertised, some benefit will accumulate to users and, by extension, to the community; if the technology fails or works differently than expected, no one is any worse for the wear. This is a false premise. As scholars attentive to various forms of digitally mediated racial discrimination and inequality have pointed out, access entails risks, costs, and benefits, all of which are unevenly distributed across existing topographies of power, across intersecting types of oppression. If we allow these power dynamics to unfold without criticism or resistance, we risk letting access provide an alibi for the harm such oppression invariably produces.

05 Access as Community Control

We want land, bread, housing, education, clothing, justice, peace and people's community control of modern technology.

HUEY NEWTON AND BOBBY SEALE, The Black Panther Party for Self-Defense Ten-Point Platform and Program

Our Stories Are Not Data

In 2018, the year I started my job as an assistant professor, I successfully applied for an in-house seed grant from my place of work, the Donald Bren School of Information and Computer Sciences at the University of California, Irvine. This grant was meant to support cutting-edge research that might be deemed too preliminary or too unorthodox for an external grant, but my intellectual approach, at least as I saw it, was firmly rooted in a time-tested approach to social informatics, the study of social aspects of computing. ICS was once known for a body of research in social informatics called the Irvine School (King, 2004). Inaugurated by the creative scholarship of Rob Kling in the 1970s, the Irvine School disputed industry hyperbole and developed nuanced understandings of the many unpredictable and surprising ways that people use computing technology. The intellectual signature of this highly varied body of work was that it was *simultaneously* critical and empirical, in that it questioned any taken-for-granted benefits of computing technology and insisted instead that the consequences of any technology had to be investigated "in vivo, inside real organizations populated by everyday people doing routine work using IT designed by regular system developers" (King, 2004, p. 99). Successors to this approach who worked at the Irvine campus in more recent decades such as Paul Dourish, Geoffrey Bowker, and Bonnie Nardi expanded the Irvine School by drawing from and contributing to social scientific and humanistic theory, placing ideas about classification, political economy, infrastructure, materiality, labor, and temporality front and center in the hands-on study of real-life technologies. In my view, these deeply influential scholars had built a reputation for the school by following the premise that there exists no social world separate from the technical sphere, a commitment shared by many researchers in science studies, human-computer interaction, communication, and education (Introna, 2006). But the term *social* had lost much of its incisiveness in the study of technology over the decades, such that the field of social informatics (and social computing and social technologies) had become stale and stubbornly apolitical. My approach, a sort of corollary to the proposition that the social is always technical and vice versa, argues that the social includes the racial. Struggles for racial justice have technological dimensions, just as the technological establishes relations of race, gender, class, citizenship, and so on.

My pitch was simple: with the support of doctoral students Benedict Olgado and Lucy Pei and undergraduate research associate Alice Lee, I wanted to bring racial justice activists who were interested in technology to campus for a conversation about their work. I did not have an exact vision of what I was trying to produce in terms of research products or publishable units, but I assumed that this project would involve my talented doctoral students and I building tools or platforms for activists. I also imagined that some direct exchange between racial justice advocates and people who hope to work in tech someday would be mutually beneficial: students in our school would learn that their work in designing interfaces, artifacts, platforms, algorithms, and models had something to do with the lived experience of working-class people of color; our community partners would encounter the enthusiastic young techies set to shape the future of the tech sector. But there was also an element of culpability and outrage fueling this intellectual project. Researchers from Irvine's leafy, suburban campus had recently contributed to the creation and normalization of powerful surveillance tools that were already being used to police, profile, and harass people in poor and working-class communities all across the United States (Heaven, 2020). I thought it important that people involved in the ongoing freedom struggles of minoritized communities get the chance to explain what it was like to live with the consequences of these technologies, to speak for themselves and their communities as experts, enjoying the authority and privileges frequently granted to academics.

I drafted a call for participation and circulated it via social media and my own professional networks. I also sought a cosponsor for the workshop, and was grateful when Yeshimabeit Milner, executive director of Data for Black Lives, "a group of activists, organizers, and mathematicians committed to the mission of using data science to create concrete and measurable change in the lives of Black people," agreed to cosponsor the event and to deliver a keynote (Data for Black Lives, n.d.). Ms. Milner, an accomplished writer and public figure, had recently convened the second Data for Black Lives meeting at the Massachusetts Institute of Technology, an influential event that attracted many scholars and technologists I admired. I was unsure who might respond, but our inaugural "Datafication and Community Activism" call reached a receptive audience of scholars, journalists, graduate students, artists, public scholars, community organizers, librarians, not-for-profit workers, and data professionals, most of whom were no doubt persuaded to attend by Ms. Milner's participation. Our first meeting included members of Data for Black Lives, The Bronx Defenders, Stop LAPD Spying Coalition, Measure, Our Data Bodies, Urban Institute, and IRISE.[1]

I had no experience programming any sort of professional event. A supportive senior colleague gave me some advice on how to run such a meeting. He suggested I dispense with stuffy introductions and formal presentations and let the invited academics get to talking right away. Scholars love to talk, he reminded me: give them the floor and they'll be happy. Uncharacteristically, I ignored this advice from a trusted mentor. Instead of offering the mic to the academics present (many of them quite senior and accomplished), I opted instead to let the community groups speak first. Our morning started with a talk by Ms. Milner entitled, "Abolish Big Data," a cogent and rousing critique of how contemporary digital technologies of data aggregation, analysis, and visualization contribute to harm in Black communities (Milner, 2019). Her talk was both technically precise and morally compelling and gave the whole rest of the workshop a direction and tenor.

Following up on the powerful inspiration Ms. Milner had provided for everything that followed, we invited our nonacademic guests to briefly and informally talk about their work and what it had to do with data via a few simple prompts. Unsurprisingly, the invited guests were gifted at public speaking and at connecting to an audience. We spent an entire day hearing the representatives of these different groups talk about how their work incorporated data and, to my surprise, how they felt great ambivalence toward digital technologies. In the day and a half that followed, we took up many important questions that we all cared about in one way or another, but that we had never heard brought together in exactly this way before. There was something new about it, a kind of family resemblance in these different dimensions of engagement with digital data. There were PowerPoints and slide shows certainly, but there were also guided meditations, physical exercises, conversations, banter, conviviality. We looked at code, data, spreadsheets, blog posts, maps, photos, charts, videos, dashboards, graphs, and letters, all manner of wonderful documents and meaningful ephemera, but mostly we looked at each other.

Near the end of the first day, one of the invited guests rose to speak. She paused at the lectern in the room we were sharing, surrounded by a friendly audience, many of whom had already taken a turn as speaker. We waited for her to start talking, then waited a moment more. She seemed pained. She took a deep breath, then confided to the audience that she felt nervous standing in front of a classroom. Her confession broke the tension in the room. The audience came to her aid, shouting enthusiastic encouragement, making their care and support heard and seen. She elaborated that, as a Black woman, she found that academic environments had frequently made her feel unwelcome. Other Black women in the audience nodded in appreciation. This speaker was a thoroughly impressive woman, a "get" for the guest list who had founded and run an organization all present respected. I was taken aback that such an accomplished person could feel intimidated at all, given her many awards and national profile, as well as her standing in the community she served. Still, after that needed adjustment, her charm, her expertise, and her gift for oratory jumped out. Over the course of twenty minutes, she articulated a vision of how data work could support Black liberation and how such a vision is grounded in the long history of activist uses of data, including the career of Ida B. Wells. She spoke of how the expertise of the community itself could be reflected in data, how data might support the authentic and expert knowledge of trusted elders and community members. That a person possessed of such obvious intellect and capacities of genuine leadership might feel threatened or unsupported in a campus environment shook me. I was not naive, nor was I a stranger to racism in the halls of academia, but I had never seen so concretely how academic environments can make it hard for some people to speak, regardless of the gravitas and eloquence of the speaker. In both her response to the stultifying aspects of academic environments and her hopes for datalogical dimensions of shared political struggle, she gave powerful voice to what many in the room were feeling but had not yet found a means of expressing. Our academic guests never really got the floor after that, but we did not notice.

Despite many wonderful moments of genuine connection, there was no real accord over what "community activism" is and how authentic, shared concerns might be represented via digital data. There were, in fact, heated conflicts, some of which provoked ill feeling or discomfort. None of these conflicts, even those that lasted past the meeting, turned on the personality or character of any single person present. These conflicts concerned parochialism, cooperation with police, academic complicity (Stop LAPD

Spying Coalition & Free Radicals, 2020), structural violence, attribution of intellectual labor, shared authorship, misogynoir (Bailey, 2021), and many other complex, interrelated issues. Some of the harsh castigations directed at me by our community partners bruised my ego, but I later came to think of these flare-ups as a kind of healthy boundary-setting. The mixture of affirmations and conflicts the meeting engendered showed me that no single event—and certainly no tool, platform, or interface—could, on its own, guarantee anyone's freedom.[2] Only sustained struggle with willing partners to think through difficult questions could move us closer to genuine solidarity and significant action.

Admonished by our community partners to "start where you are," I came away from that first meeting with a greater understanding of how higher education, like public education and like the tech sector, is wrapped up with the systems and hierarchies that mark some communities as deserving and others as bereft and reprobate (Pierre et al., 2021). Academia is a site of many interlocking forms of oppression and the credentials it produces are highly valued in other powerful racialized institutions and organizations (Ray, 2019), including the technology-focused private corporations that constitute most of the tech sector. I recognized that the most spirited and cogent critiques of academia's role in structural oppression came from community organizers, who were also highly critical of other kinds of actors, including not-for-profits and community-based organizations. Community organizing based in working-class communities of color emerged as an important source of grassroots power and astute criticism of oppressive tendencies in other organizations. Moreover, many community organizers were already deeply engaged with the accumulation and circulation of digital data, and had been for some time.

In starting the workshop, I was looking for a way to describe the relationship between minoritized communities and datafication, but the Evoke Lab ended up with a slightly different approach, which was to build relationships with people who were already involved in movement work, particularly community organizers. In other words, the thing I was thinking about was not an existing fact out in the world, but was itself a kind of practice that people can do together, tentatively, haltingly, with no guarantee of success. Over the years, our strategy has prioritized listening to our colleague so that we might be educated about how digital data in all of its forms and manifestations relates to the self-determination and ongoing freedom struggles of working-class communities of color. To date, we have been fortunate to work with many national and regional organizations who are generally interested in digital data but are specifically concerned with civic education, abolition of police, racial discrimination in computational systems, data-driven government services, reintegration of formerly incarcerated people, economic empowerment, and many other issues of interest to working-class communities of color. These technological aspects of community organizing play out in very surprising ways, especially where the overtly political and social movement-aligned work of community organizing intersects with the pleasures and potentials of digital data. But before I describe some of what organizers do with data, it's important to visit a caution I have heard from organizers again and again over the years. In a collective writing produced at the first Datafication and Community Activism workshop, our participants wrote, "Data can be used to tell stories, but our stories are not data" (Datafication and Community Activism Workshop, 2019).

Spreadsheets for Racial Justice

The commonsensical appeal of access to technology can be deployed at any scale or level of analysis. Individual people need access to technology, especially if they are poor, or working-class, or in any way disadvantaged in economic life. Organizations like public schools can also cast their programmatic interventions and pedagogical experiments in terms of access: kids need technology to build digital literacy, get into college, prepare for the workforce, engage in twenty-first-century learning, or any other scheme that relates to accomplishing desirable futures or, more to the point, avoiding the threats to freedom, life, and flourishing that are placed before people born in minoritized communities. Whole communities themselves can be rendered as bereft and, therefore, in need of access to technology: this vision is frequently pursued by Black philanthropists and technologists themselves. Access is voracious; its social justice implications can be levied at continental scale and even global scale: AI for Africa relies on this logic, but so do philanthropic arms of the tech sector who aim to provide for-profit computational resources to "the next billion" wired citizens, most of them women of color in the Global South (de Bastion & Mukku, 2020).

In the previous chapters, I showed how a call for social justice in the form of access to technology played out in schools and organizations that serve working-class communities of color: more edtech meant more data, not necessarily any significant change or improvement in the quality of public education. In addition, working with data conferred strategic, rhetorical, and reputational advantages to certain actors, but these advantages did not inhere in the community itself: they could not. School administrators could give their activities a veneer of objectivity, even when the data they had was gibberish. A charter management organization could mask its discredited, deficit-informed educational strategies in code and data visualization, dressing itself up in tech sector drag. Those who worked most closely with technology understood these dynamics at some level, and adopted a variety of stances or tactics in response to these efforts to make data into a tool to shape reality. But within working-class communities of color themselves, there are forms of collective resistance that also engage with data and data-drivenness, although to drastically different ends and via varied, sometimes conflictual means. Technology has powerful reputational appeal, but there are those who question technology and in doing so, find ways to thwart, subvert, redirect, snub, escape, or knowingly tolerate the extractive relations offered by the tech sector's advance into public services such as education. Even as the longed-for social justice virtues of access to technology (at the scale of the classroom, the school, the city) set the stage for extractive relations, it is vital to remember that these relations are always disputed and resisted, most often in stealthy, individual ways, but sometimes in organized, legible, coherent ways. One place to look for traces of these nuanced, furtive, and frequently covert kinds of resistance to technological power is in the work of community organizers.

This chapter pivots conceptually, to highlight the work of community organizers who are working with, through, and against datafication.[3] Community organizing represents a coordinated effort to get at the root inequality of American public life, including the use of education technology in public schools. Conceptually, thinking about how community organizers adapt to the expectations and political possibilities of datafication lets us revise the beleaguered virtue of access to technology by anchoring it in terms, concepts, and tactics created by and in conversation with working-class communities of color, both in the past and in the present.[4] This approach certainly departs from research on education technology and public life, but that is precisely the leap I am asking readers, researchers, and the broader public to make.

Organizing is a common feature of American political life (e.g., labor unions, major and minor political parties, private interest groups, ethnic or religious organizations, issue campaigns). Community organizing concerns building grassroots power, especially in minoritized communities. Community organizing refers to both a philosophy of social or political change and to whatever techniques of direct political action might be deployed in pursuit of such a philosophy. Like many other kinds of political actors, community organizers can engage in electoral politics, but they also frequently act outside the electoral system through protest, coalition building, lawsuits, and community education (Christens & Dolan, 2011). Community organizers, through collective action, solidarity, and mobilization, seek to change, shape, or alter the material conditions of the people in the communities they serve, regardless of whether the larger polity recognizes their rights or dignity.

As both a playbook of tactics and a coherent democratic ethos, community organizing holds that regular people can, at certain opportune junctures, shape public life to promote collective change. These tactics might take the form of spectacle or protest, but they might also encompass mass communications, community education, art, or simply taking up space. Needless to say, this whole gamut of tactics and philosophy spans many conflictual and incommensurable commitments about digital technology and its ability to address community needs, including approaches that view data-intensive technologies as always fundamentally harmful to minoritized communities and those that hope to use technology for community-defined aims (Dencik et al., 2022; Gray, 2018; Milan & van der Velden, 2016). Community organizers might create, aggregate, and visualize data in order to inform organizational activities, agitate for policy, and drive public opinion; but they also frequently criticize via their work the design, development, and use of data-intensive technologies in a variety of domains, including law enforcement, public education, public health, and child welfare (Crooks & Currie, 2021; Eubanks, 2017).

Community organizing is also a job, one increasingly undertaken by skilled and educated workers inspired by movement goals and employed by overtly political groups, including many not-for profit, civil society organizations.[5] Like many other forms of work, community organizing has become increasingly datafied, executed via the commercial tools and platforms used in all kinds of professions. But for community organizers, data work is not just about data: it is about meaningful attempts to change the world, largely through storytelling and building relationships. Community organizers who live or work in minoritized communities use many forms of data and digital platforms, but this engagement with data differs in important ways from the public and public-facing organizations explored earlier in this book. These organizers recognize the tactical value of expressing community goals via the creation, circulation, or consultation of data, but these uses of data can undercut the larger ethos of community organizing in important and painful ways. Accordingly, data achieves a curious duality that can trap unwary organizers: it provides a limited, provisional, and potentially powerful avenue of directing attention to movement goals, but it is also one of the means by which the state accomplishes the minoritization of working-class communities of color in the first place. Digital data, like other forms of digital technology, is an end unto itself (Introna, 2006), and this fact makes its political deployment unpredictable and complicated.

The use of digital data for political goals by community organizers in working class communities of color poses a classic double bind, a situation in which an "agent is given two (or perhaps more) injunctions as to how to behave, and these injunctions conflict, so that it is not possible to fulfill both of them" (Jenkins, 2014). First, the kind of technical expertise needed to create, aggregate, and visualize digital data is largely concentrated in elite spaces of knowledge production: tech companies, universities, think tanks, research centers, and government institutions. Community organizers, particularly those working for the benefit of minoritized communities, are less likely to have had chances to learn technical skills related to data analysis and have encountered more obstacles in following career trajectories and educational pathways that confer such expertise (McGee, 2020). Many of the organizers we work with, even those whose jobs turn specifically on the creation, aggregation, or analysis of digital data questioned their own expertise relative to both stereotypical images of tech workers (white, nerdy, male, STEM-credentialed) and relative to more objective markers of expertise, such as the technical skills listed in tech-focused job ads. To be clear, there certainly exist highly skilled individuals and technologically savvy organizations that work in this space, some of them quite well-known and prominent in academia and national media. But the organizers we have interviewed most often distinguish their kind of data work as being executed via common, free-to-use tools and off-the-shelf platforms.

Second, data work threatens to sap community resources, especially the time and labor of community organizers via the same dynamics of capture detailed earlier in this book. Expending time, labor, and expertise on the platforms and tools that are needed to do data work can represent a real redirection of limited resources, all of which produce value for the tech sector. As McGee points out, the tech sector, including STEM higher education, is itself built on "Eurocentric," sexist ideologies that effectively limit the participation of women and people of color. (McGee, 2020, p. 635). Moreover, the organizers we are working with are not interested in supporting the tech sector: they are trying to use whatever tools are at hand for authentic community work, even as they recognize that the commercial tools and platforms they use turn their work into a potential vector of surveillance and an asset that pays someone else.

Thirdly, the benefits of data work tend to benefit those who are best positioned by power, prestige, and wealth to reap its benefits (Heeks & Shekhar, 2019). Coleman (2017) makes a similar point when discussing the political projects of technical elites. When hackers use the "weapons of the geek" for favored political projects, the result is that the concerns of those who are already members of the cultural and economic elite are given new means to pursue their interests. A similar dynamic obtains here as well; those who are already positioned by wealth or social capital to acquire technical skills get an outsize role in determining what ends and means political projects should focus on. As our community partners and allies insist, belief in the power of data can turn into fetishism and superstition. Data can be a useful strategy for making a point or for getting an institution to move, but data is not the point of anything: the point is to build power in the community.

Summing up, this "double bind" of datalogical enframing of the political aspirations of minoritized peoples, what community organizers are interested in can sometimes be expressed as data or can incorporate data as a tactic, but cannot be satisfied via any glib technocenterism. As I have argued with respect to the use of data in public schools (and by extension, in other kinds of government service), data is not out in the world waiting to give up its patterns: it is given meaning, a meaning that is frequently contested and disputed. Interpreting or reinterpreting data is another field of contestation, not some apolitical arena where the world itself (via the mimetic captures of data) will settle disputes in human affairs. Organizers know this: they do not allow that data is out there ready to obviate the need for struggle. Instead, organizers cannily use data (and the reputational benefits it carries with it) and deploy that power for their own purposes. It is a tactical response to the datalogical enframing of expert organizations, a way to use an infatuation with data against those centers of power that always seem to benefit from data-drivenness.

The approaches we have seen among community organizers in the present stretch back to a lineage of struggle for a more free, more democratic American public. The Movement for Black Lives, typified by the circulation of the #BlackLivesMatter hashtag in 2013, represents "a renewed, insurgent orientation toward Black politics, protest, and political thought, chiefly but not exclusively among younger Black folks" (Harris, 2023, p. 5). As Sarah Jackson and others have written, the Movement for Black Lives made effective use of contemporary social media to circulate ideas shaped by feminist thought (Jackson, 2016), but it also drew on longer traditions of purposive witnessing of anti-Black violence by journalists and everyday people (Richardson, 2020). Certainly, such witnessing can be traced back to a time before the rise of contemporary regimes of data-intensive computation and the valorization of digital data as a proxy for all forms of human activity (or to a time before the invention of mechanical computers full stop). At the close of the nineteenth century (as our colleague from the first Datafication and Community Activism workshop reminded us), Ida Bell Wells-Barnett publicized the extra-judicial killings of Black people via lynching by publishing tables documenting the details of these cases and pairing them with graphic descriptions of violence in her 1895 pamphlet *The Red Record*. The form of her quantitative descriptions—tabular, seemingly objective, factual—formed a harsh rebuke of the banality of lynching, how common and tolerated such spectacular mob violence was during the period of her research. Quite shrewdly, the seemingly static and flat facticity of such murders irrefutably supported a political argument, namely that such lynchings amounted to state-sanctioned crimes against Black Americans that should be stopped by the intervention of legal authorities. In a similar vein, Battle-Baptiste and Rusert (2018) show how the long history of Black activism in the United States connects uses of data in the previous century to contemporary social movements, including the Black Lives Matter movement, prison abolitionists, environmental justice advocates, and other contemporary struggles that touch working-class communities of color. Their careful historical work contextualizes a series of data visualizations produced by W. E. B. Du Bois for the 1900 Paris Exposition, a world's fair staged in Paris, France, that featured displays and exhibits by exhibitors from over forty contributing nations, colonies, and territories. As the authors note, Du Bois's "data portraits"—an extensive set of colorful data visualizations, maps, charts, and graphs—deployed graphical conventions that would be familiar to contemporary viewers as well as a number of artistic interventions and lettering effects unique to the period in service of a singular narrative: the multifaceted story of Black experience dating to the abolition of slavery. This narrative, constructed through quantitative facts, told a story of Black economic and social improvement and carried with it a political message to twentieth-century viewers: Black people in the United States could form thriving communities in the absence of legalized slavery, lynching, and discrimination. In other words, Du Bois argued that Black abjection was caused by state violence, not by the innate inferiority of Black people. There are many forebears who have inspired the uses of data by minoritized communities in the United States for expressly political purposes, but in the next section, I want to go back to a moment when Black activists intervened in the provision of public services and incorporated this program into a criticism of contemporary technologies, a criticism I will use to show how contemporary organizers get around the double bind of working with tech sector tools and platforms.

People's Community Control of Technology

Just as Alondra Nelson (2011) looked to the Black Panther Party's community health programs to better understand contemporary public health conflicts and their racial implications in her seminal work *Body and Soul: The Black Panther Party and the Fight against Medical Discrimination*, I likewise look to the Panthers to understand the current confluence of race, digital data, community organizing, and public education. As Nelson describes the Black Panther Party's approach to what some contemporary organizers might call health justice, the party took up matters of concern to Black Americans that challenged the racial hierarchy of public life through contestations that were both practical and ideational (Nelson, 2011, p. xii). By calling back to the work of the Black Panther Party and its particular mode of radical resistance to state-sponsored oppression, we can see how demands for access themselves can be transformative and more tightly linked to a project of racial and social justice. This path requires a different way of thinking through the raced and highly charged relations offered by a datafied public sphere that accounts for material needs but looks beyond the mere distribution of needed goods and services. As working-class people of color themselves have frequently insisted (in the course of the research for this book and elsewhere), material concerns are central to demands for liberation, but liberation and access are not equivalent, coextensive, or substitutable. The intellectual and programmatic work of the Black Panther Party during the party's most active and successful period in the late 1960s and early 1970s offers no simple solutions, but instead encourages more critical and more pointed questioning about what public life demands and how it might be entered into more equitably by those minoritized peoples and communities whose lesser status is built into both the most fundamental mechanisms of the state and its ambition to remake public service in the image of the tech sector.

To briefly sketch that moment, the Black Panther Party for Self-Defense (BPP), founded in 1966 in Oakland, California, by Huey P. Newton and Bobby Seale, came about to offer armed resistance to police brutality in Black communities. The BPP articulated its aims via the Ten-Point Program, which functioned as both an organizing tool and a manifesto. The group was formed amid a turn toward more militant civil rights protest, as distinguished from an earlier phase of the U.S. civil rights movement centered on nonviolent mass protest as a response to legalized, Jim Crow segregation. This later stage of Black political organizing, sometimes called Black Nationalism or Black Power, relocated the most publicized sites of Black American political struggle away from the South. This movement occurred against the backdrop of the assassination of Malcolm X and the Watts Rebellion, two key events that changed the strategy of political organizations and highlighted the violent repression of Black political activism. Frustrated with the slow pace of government responses to civil rights agitation and lackluster public support for racial equality, many young people came to the view that Black participation in the American public should be determined by Black people themselves. Many politically active people at the time came to conclude that the institutions that made up the public—the military, public schools, higher education—were predicated on and contributed to Black oppression. Liberation for Black people would not come from a state founded on and dedicated to racism and exploitation, but from Black communities organizing themselves to provide for the material, political, and intellectual needs of their own people. This more confrontational, liberation-focused approach directly inspired other minoritized communities (e.g., the Brown Berets) via its dual approach: political critique and a practical set of community services. The BPP faced constant surveillance, harassment, entrapment, and violence from various law enforcement agencies, including the FBI's COINTELPRO, whose years-long effort to discredit and entrap BPP members (including the spectacular public acquittal of the Panther 21 in 1971) deeply wounded the party and limited its long-term survival.

In terms of the political commitments if its leaders, BPP's political perspective, informed heavily by the works of Mao Zedong and Frantz Fanon, synthesized a largely Marxist framework for understanding Black political activism. BPP writings depicted American public life as irredeemably wrapped up with violence, extraction, and enclosure. Especially via the incendiary and widely circulated text and oratory of founders Newton and Seale (and their frequent targeting by law enforcement and government), BPP philosophy linked the simultaneous oppression of Asian peoples abroad—via the imperial war in Vietnam—and Black oppression domestically—via discrimination, criminalization, and segregation. The solution to this system of oppression and imperialism was for the collective economic independence and political self-determination of Black communities. This critique was in many respects out of sync with the political views of a majority of Black Americans at the time, who largely supported integrationist reforms and other incremental change (Alkebulan, 2007).

As opposed to their political philosophies, BPP community programs were more widely accepted and popular. Due in part to the contributions of Stokely Carmichael (Kwame Ture), who joined the party after leading the Student Nonviolent Coordinating Committee, the BPP, especially after 1970, focused more intently on its mission to include provision of community services, particularly in arenas where the state had shirked its obligations toward Black communities such as health, voting, and education. The BPP developed "survival programs," a community-based model that called on active party members to engage in commercial activity (e.g., selling newspapers) that would support community projects, such as the Panther's health centers and free breakfast programs. These programs were aimed at materially improving the collective life of the communities where party members lived, capturing the value of Black labor for the shared benefit of Black people themselves. BPP leadership required local chapters to provide community services, including voter drives and educational programs. From 1973 to 1982, the BPP ran what came to be called the Oakland Community School, an experimental day school that incorporated community-based learning, service, political education, and life skills training in its curriculum. Via their educational offerings, the Panthers articulated a cogent critique of the role of public education, even supposedly racially integrated public education, in training young people in the ideology of U.S. imperialism at home and abroad and, perhaps most strategically, modeled an alternative. The Oakland School, as well as the Panther's efforts to feed, house, clothe, transport, and heal were authentically developed for the benefit of Black communities, provided by resources internal to Black communities, and based on the self-defined needs of Black communities. It was a concretized vision of a particularist collective life, one that did not hide or obscure difference in the name of a false universalism, a fully realized way of creating "the conditions of possibility for a free life for all, without misery or oppression" (Gordon, 2017, p. 200).

By 1972, the party was hemmed up, politically and economically compromised by violent attacks by police, court cases, surveillance, and infiltration from the outside, as well as interpersonal conflict, political differences, sexism, and disagreements over strategy from the inside. At this time, the party added "Community Control of Modern Technology" to the tenth point in in the Ten-Point Program, so that the amended text read "We want land, bread, housing, education, clothing, justice, peace and people's community control of modern technology" (as quoted in Alkebulan [2007]). As historians of the BPP and memoirs of surviving leaders attest, this turn represented a fundamental rethinking of leading BPP intellectual Huey Newton away from armed resistance. In Newton's view, U.S. imperialism had entered a new stage where armed revolt by Black communities, even aided by international allies, would be futile (Narayan, 2020). Newton predicted that communist states all over the world would be seduced by the appeal of consumer society and be incorporated into global regimes of capitalist production. At the same time, "the interests of corporate capital, technological advancement and a new geography of industrial production would lead to deindustrialization, precarious employment, welfare state retrenchment, and an orgy of profit in the First World" (p. 196). This turn in BPP philosophy, shorthanded by Panther Chairwoman Elaine Brown as "the technology question" accurately predicted many transformations in the global capitalism of the late twentieth century. Newton thought the emerging shape of the world economic system required new or drastically reordered institutions based on shared, liberatory values (Narayan, 2020, p. 200).

This later recognition of "the technology question" in the BPP's core demands can provide a few important directions for thinking through the relationship of contemporary organizers, the state, and technology. First, this perhaps lesser-known aspect of Panther philosophy shows that Black political theorists have already contributed significantly to the political economy of contemporary technology, what it is, what it can do, and how it shapes democratic life. "The technology question" points to the power of technology and its character as a tool of global capital. In this respect, there is nothing automatically emancipatory, creative, or collectively meaningful to uses of technology: this critique foregrounds the voraciousness and mobility of capital and the capture of the apparatus of the state as capital's enforcer. It is a grim view of technology, but one that provides a needed counterweight to the ability of tech sector hype to dictate the terms by which researchers understand technology itself. This move also indicates the primacy of accounts of material conditions to understanding past and liberatory movements and contemporary social movements alike.

Second, "the technology question" points to a stinging critique of state violence. Later BPP philosophy argued that party members should seek to transform public institutions where possible (a tactic familiar to earlier civil rights movement groups such as the Student Nonviolent Coordinating Committee). This move to take over institutions, seek office, and participate in electoral politics was rejected by some leaders and party members as assimilationist, but the message for contemporary readers is clear: the state may be controlled by economic and cultural elites, but it can be tamed, shaped, or resisted at key points. Some regimes are more violent than others, and the difference between these regimes will mean life or death for people targeted by state violence. People who want to survive state violence look for moments where the apparatus of power is vulnerable, then act in coordinated, collective ways to curb the power of the state to harm, enclose, and kill. The BPP critique makes clear that the first order of business is survival, followed by the far-off goal of some change that will bring freedom for all people. The idea of armed revolt and exodus was motivating and effective, but it was also fantastical and ahistorical. There can be no return to some communal life outside, prior to, exterior to this world, because we are already here, where we have always been. It is this collective entity, in its expansive wisdom and endless tenacity, that promises the power to shape a different state and a different world.

Third, the technology question also provides directions for the accomplishment of this freedom in the form of "people's community control of technology," a collective approach to questions of technological agency. In this formulation, "people's community control" implies access to needed technologies on a coequal status with other material needs (food, clothing, housing), but it also marks a sense of managing where technology goes and what it can be allowed to do. It asserts a power above technology, a collective power that would decide on matters of concern to the group. To think of this historical vision as a demand for technologies not yet in existence that enact, embody, or promote shared, democratic governance at every scale and mode of life for all people is to recognize how terribly small the imagination of both public life and digital technologies have become.

"People's community control of technology" serves as the entry point for an exploration of how contemporary community organizers have used and resisted data-intensive computation in their ongoing struggles for racial equality. An interest in the use of data shapes the practices of community organizers, just as it shapes the practices of data professionals elsewhere. However, organizers based in working-class communities of color share professional, political, and intellectual commitments that mark their work with data. This distinction is important not just because it allows this book to valorize the work of organizers, but also because it shows an extant but underappreciated way of thinking about technology that arises from minoritized communities themselves.

Three Dimensions of Community Control

In what follows, I want to broadly sketch out some common dimensions of data practices as described by subjects of research interviews in light of the term *people's community control of modern technology*. To be clear, when organizers talked about their work, this was not a term that they used. But what I want to show with this characterization of data practices is that despite clichéd invocations of newness, novelty, and innovation so common to technological discourse, the organizers I am interested in here are also working within established intellectual, aesthetic, and political traditions. These organizers care about access to technology, but only insofar as such access contributes to community goals.

To do this work, my team at the Evoke Lab first interviewed those organizers with whom we already had existing relationships. Then we recruited more widely via personal introduction, word of mouth, and social media. Our only criterion for recruitment was that the respondent had to be a professional community organizer. We asked these self-identified professional community organizers to describe the particulars of their work using fairly standard interview questions typical of research on occupations: who they worked for, how long they had been so employed, and what kind of job history and educational qualifications they brought to this work. We also asked questions about tools and platforms and looked at code or other samples of work when possible, a research strategy I had used to learn about the work of data professionals in previous chapters. We recorded and transcribed our interviews, then looked across all of our collected conversations to draw out some themes via qualitative coding. While this research is ongoing at the time of writing, some clear tendencies among our respondents have emerged over the last three years. We have interviewed roughly fifty organizers so far; the vast majority of them live, work, and serve working-class communities of color in the United States, mostly in California.

While nearly all of our respondents described data as "important" or "very important" to the work of community organizing, we found that work with data hewed to distinct patterns for those organizers working in minoritized communities. These organizers described pressures to collect, maintain, and consult data, but they were quick to point out that such skills were secondary to the most important aspect of this kind of work, which is the maintenance of relationships. As one of our respondents put it, community organizing is both art and science: the impetus to work with digital data and other digital tools and platforms speaks to the science of organizing, but the art of community organizing, the most vital and important part, is in relationships. Our respondents spoke of the intricate, nuanced, and purposive ways that organizers use data to relate to themselves, to their communities, to other organizations, and to the state (Pei et al., 2022). We noted among organizers a certain sense of technical inadequacy (similar again to the sense of lesser competence relative to industry norms and media depictions of techies I noted among some data professionals and educators earlier in this book). As one organizer whose work involved managing a database about environmental justice issues assembled from public records put it, "I am not a data scientist. I don't collect data personally; I bumble around in Excel. . . . I'm not going to beat Google at its own game."

In terms of its political potential beyond the demands of datafied office work, organizers expressly did not view data as a means to gather evidence to support better, more democratic government action or public consensus: data was an agonistic tool, one crafted to build commitment, solidarity, and power within the community itself (Crooks & Currie, 2021). Digital technologies confer authority and reputational benefits, so it makes sense that these organizers would, by nature of their desire to shape and wield community power, make use of that tool (or any tool that could promise similar benefits, for that matter). We found several different scenarios where community organizers used digital data in their political work, but reliance on data had to be tempered with concerns for relationships and movement goals—in short, for community control. Below, I sketch out briefly how community control is effected by organizers via refusal, receipts, and respect.

Refusal

Somewhat regularly, a community partner or potential interview subject has rebuffed our requests for collaboration. Organizers we want to work with don't always state the reason why they decline to participate, but when they have offered explanations, we frequently hear that organizers want to be paid more for their expertise, that they do not wish to divulge their tactics, and that they don't trust academic researchers. We have heard, more than once, some version of the expression "Nothing about us without us." Organizers are (rightfully) suspicious of academic researchers, who have tended to appropriate the work of organizers and repackaged it as research. Because community organizers operate in public and circulate materials they have created for purposes of community education, their work, including maps, databases, infographics, and writing, has been reused by journalists, scholars, not-for-profits, or even other organizers, often without citation (Pierre et al., 2021). We have found even in these seemingly fleeting encounters a strategy of refusal, a purposeful tactic of avoiding the datalogical enframing of community concerns, a way to avoid giving in to calculative powers that seek to capture community work as data.

Refusal as both an empirically observed tactic and a theoretically generative concept has featured prominently in anthropology and feminist approaches to critical data studies (Barabas, 2022; Cifor et al., 2019; D'Ignazio & Klein, 2023; McGranahan, 2016; Simpson, 2007). For minoritized subjects, whose unequal status with respect to state and to powerful institutions such as the university are justified via representational systems, refusal becomes a charged, aesthetic, and lively practice, not simply a rejection of a request or demand. The political anthropologist Audra Simpson writes of the complexities of her ethnographic study of her own people, the Kahnawà:ke Mohawk Nation, by making analytical and theoretical use of refusal. She argues that her fellow community members' evasiveness about certain questions of sovereignty not only disputes particular kinds of reductive representations of native peoples, but undercuts representation by colonial agencies all together (Simpson, 2007). Such refusal activates a series of affective states and shared lexicons, a collective sense of rebellious freedom among political allies and fellow community members. As one of our research subjects explained it, her earliest entry into the world of community organizing came in a gleeful moment of refusal:

> I say that I started as an organizer in eighth grade. I led a walkout of school because I had a teacher that was on some bullshit. Like he was racist, and I was like, okay we're not staying in this class. We're going to walk out; we're going to refuse to go back to this class. I feel like that was my first organizing experience.

Refusal as it relates to data, then, is the rejection of representation. Organizers warned our research team that the relationship between the community and data that supposedly represented it could often be strained or even unworkable. It was not the case that organizers assumed that data could mimetically reflect aspects of the community's life and that they could then serve that data up to some platform or apparatus unproblematically. From the outset, organizers were suspicious of data work and technical expertise. So the first and best option in many cases would be to refuse to collect, share, or circulate data all together. These concerns were also tied up with practical concerns about infiltration of groups and surveillance by police.

In terms of the day-to-day work of community organizing, refusal has particular significance for undocumented people, an important constituency of many of the organizers we interviewed. These organizers described data work that refused certain kinds of data collection about community members. For example, an organizer who worked on food insecurity and mutual aid for houseless people shared that although his organization could have gathered more resources for their free grocery pop-up if they collected data on the community members who came to get food, this would pose a risk for undocumented community members. His refusal to collect data meant that undocumented community members would be protected and able to continue getting groceries:

> We actually fight against some data collection. One of the things that happened with food distribution [is that] we have really avoided most of the traditional venues for getting food to distribute because they require some data collection. . . . They want you to collect demographic data, they want you to check IDs. A lot of times, it's limited to like you have to live in a certain zip code to access the services. And we just refuse to do that. We're like, you're hungry, come and get food. We don't care about any of that.

Respect

Community organizers devoted significant time in our interviews to the lived experience of community members or, more to the point, to making sure that data did not become privileged over the wisdom and experience held collectively in the community. Organizers recognized a certain incommensurability in data, one that frustrated them, but did not dissuade them entirely from data work: data could be useful, but it should not be taken as a substitute for the valid, important knowledge of community members. It was common for our interview subjects to insist that digital data presented a partial and privileged way of knowing, one that only confirmed what people in the community already knew from living through issues such as homelessness, over-policing, and disinvestment. Spending the time and energy to create, collect, or circulate data about what everybody already knew in the hopes that not-for-profits or the government would pay attention struck a lot of our respondents as misguided.

On the other hand, some organizers valued the importance of being represented in data as a way to underscore or validate community knowledge. One organizer who worked on youth organizing and police abolition, for example, warned us that data alone could not capture the community's experience of police violence, which included the names of people killed by police, eyewitness descriptions of the killing, impact statements by survivors of the deceased, and ongoing agitation for justice, redress, and accountability (Pierre et al., 2021). While data that represented the number of people killed by police in the community or the number of people shot by a particular officer might be tactically important, especially for getting journalists and academics to write about these killings, the organizer warned our team that such data was only a partial aspect of the truth. For this organizer, the story of the killing had to include the victim, the survivors, the perpetrators, the lack of legal consequences, and the community's mobilization. Moreover, this organizer insisted that numbers and stories together better approached the truth of what people in the community were experiencing: not an isolated killing, but a more complex experience of loss, grief, trauma, resignation, and, ultimately, collective response.

Organizers shared that they needed to build trust to be accepted *within* the community and also *as* representatives of the community in political doings. The community organizers we interviewed pointed to specific and situated ways of evaluating the needs of their communities and developing nuanced and tactical ways of working with data. These tactics varied according to the larger political interests of organizers (for example, what kind of campaign of organization they worked for and what goals they were working toward), but in total, they recognized sophisticated ways of thinking about community. These organizers were characteristically ambivalent about data work: they recognized its utility and potential significance, but they always cautioned us about letting data stand in for the great variety of people, situations, motivations, and relationships that constituted the communities they served. As one organizer described this dynamic,

> Yeah, I think data can [be useful], there are always risks. What is the word, generalizability, right? You can generalize the population, and that can be harmful on them. . . . Also I think data currently, notions of objectivity are favored over subjectivity, which I think can be harmful, because I believe in the power of storytelling, and how our experience is also data.

Receipts

A common form of data work we saw among the organizers we interviewed concerned working with public records, administrative data, or other kinds of government information. Data is the means by which city, state, county, federal, and international governments "see," how they direct their activities and determine their efficacy, but also how they understand, delimit, and govern the polity (Porter, 1996; Scott, 1998). Unsurprisingly, community organizers active in trying to limit harms related to government or state-funded actions in their communities deployed data to talk back to those individuals and institutions charged with making policy. But this dialogue was halting, uneven, and heated, not a cool debate among reasoned positions based on objective evidence, but an affectively charged battle between competing narratives. By far, most of the organizers had hostile relationships with elected and unelected officials. Data collected by these organizers was frequently shared to resist, discredit, or expose aspects of policy (or personal behavior) that organizers found harmful to their communities. Most of the organizers we worked with deeply distrusted any state-funded organization, preferring instead to rely on community networks of support (e.g., mutual aid).

Data work among organizers focused on telling stories about the community in ways that would support the work of other not-for-profit or public service organizations. In terms of the reward structure of professional community organizing itself, funders formed a particularly important organizational audience. All of the community organizers we talked to worked in the not-for-profit sector, either for a large organization that employed organizers or for a smaller, community-based organization that might depend on funds from a larger not-for-profit on a project-by-project basis. So among all the organizers we interviewed, a common audience for the outputs of data work had to do with communicating with larger organizations. These larger, better-funded, more established organizations frequently demanded forms of data in exchange for operating funds, salaries, and other financial resources. Funders often required extensive data sharing, so much so that for one organizer we interviewed, concerns about the surveillance of community members bothered her. The data that funders were most frequently interested in concerned contact with community members who could be mobilized for direct political actions: voting, certainly, but also protests, meetings, or workshops. Potentially, contacts at one site or organization could be converted or mobilized by another organizer: this aspect of the work of community organizers was so obvious to many of our interviewees that they had to be prompted to acknowledge that such an outcome was the point of much of their work. One interviewee shared that before putting together a proposal for a new project, she collected data about the community and its conditions and reported this to her funders. This description, created using publicly available data, served as the basis for her budget requests. This aspect of her work, the background data collection, was in some way the price of entry for an audience with the larger organization that acted as funder. Likewise, institutional funders require data and follow-up reports after funding a project.

Finally, local officials (both elected and unelected) were frequently a presumed audience of data work, although such work almost always reached this audience through public channels or social media. Presumably, community organizers who are explicitly interested in policy outcomes would consider communicating their data work to the makers and administrators of such policy, but this relationship was the site of antagonism and tension from nearly every community organizer we interviewed.

Organizers frequently demanded information from the state to then use that data to legitimize their preferred policies to the broader public, courts, lawmakers at other levels of government, or other kinds of elected officials more sympathetic to the community. This amounted to using data produced by one arm of the state to try to coerce some other arm. For example, some organizers we interviewed used Freedom of Information Act requests to get information about police budgets, especially expenditures on technology. They then used this data to support claims that working-class communities of color are over-policed, that police expenditures on technology did not increase public safety, and that vendors had enriched themselves unjustly through sales of discredited or unproven technologies (many of them touted as data-driven, ironically). This kind of engagement with state-produced data could then be used to write letters and create awareness among legislators around an issue, to educate community members, to fuel social media campaigns, or to embarrass or intimidate specific politicians or departments. In this capacity, community organizers' use of data was characterized with less ambivalence, but even in cases where data provided strong evidentiary claims to inspire, force, or resist specific policies, tensions remained. As one respondent put it,

> We know this data is being collected, but governmental agencies are really good at hiding that . . . by not having it visible. . . . The only way they could get the data they wanted is they had to go to this one office in City Hall with a pencil and a notepad and copy it

down. They could not take pictures of it on their phone. It wasn't digital. It's like, come on. They would say, "Oh, this is all publicly available. Just come and get it." But the barriers are there, and sometimes you just have to push. Sometimes a push is not enough, but a threat is enough. Sometimes you have to. . . . We do the Freedom of Information Act often to get stuff because it's more likely to produce results if you're getting stonewalled.

In rare cases, legal activists used data collected this way for lawsuits aimed at local, city, county, or state agencies, although most all of the organizers we interviewed lacked the financial resources to pursue legal action in this way. So instead of using data to sway or inform the state, these organizers were providing an important counterpoint to elected officials (even those elected officials who represent minoritized communities), who were seen as beholden to the interests of financial elites. In this respect, data work was not about objectivity or reason, but about making dramatic rhetorical use of the misbehavior of powerful institutions that were assumed to be incapable or unwilling to see authentic needs within the community. On rare occasions, community organizers might use data to directly advocate for a specific policy, especially at the local and state level. We found that only a few of the grassroots organizers we interviewed tried to use data they had collected as a basis to draft bills for which they then sought sponsorship among legislators.

While these descriptions of the uses of data by community organizers—refusal, respect, and receipts—are not meant as an exhaustive taxonomy, they do give a sense of what datafication means for a small but growing group of people who are professionally engaged in social movements dedicated to the collective well-being of minoritized communities. Nearly all of the interviewees my research group has contacted are in some way working in a longer tradition of "community control," fitting contemporary digital tools into current iterations of struggle rather than letting technology subsume their shared visions of a more just future.

Conclusion

Access Is Capture (But Some of Us Get Free)

It is 2016. In the days immediately following the election of Donald Trump to the U.S. presidency, thousands of public high school students in and around South and East Los Angeles stage unauthorized demonstrations. In Hyde Park, Inglewood, South Park, Boyle Heights, Compton, and every other working-class Black and Latinx neighborhood, students tell reporters that they march to denounce deportations, homophobia, police violence, and all forms of racism, those that already exist and those that might be enshrined in law by a Trump administration. These student protestors, many of them undocumented and too young to vote, join with college students, working people, community members, everyday citizens, clergy, and local politicians in a series of walk-outs, marches, demonstrations, and protests in the aftermath of the election, some of them planned, many of them spontaneous. In recognition of the large numbers of participants and intensity of feeling caught up in these multiethnic civic actions that have cropped up all over the city, school authorities, such as the superintendent of the Los Angeles Unified School District, decline to punish students for walking out of class. In the *Los Angeles Times*, Armando Farias, deputy chief of Los Angeles School Police, a separate police force that operates exclusively in the city's public schools, says, "It's been a while. I don't remember the last time we had something . . . of this magnitude" (Kohli et al., 2016).

It is 2018. Akila Robinson and Kelly Hernandez, students at Secondary School of Journalism in Brooklyn, New York, tell an education blog's reporter about a walk-out they organized to protest the use of edtech at their school (Sullivan, 2019). Their high school, which scores lower than the state average on common metrics of school quality concerning graduation, standardized tests, and college matriculation, has largely replaced instruction with a platform enthusiastically supported by private philanthropic investment, Summit Learning. Students report a number of familiar IT problems: they don't have enough laptops for all students, the wireless network cannot support so many connections, they have lost their log-ins and passwords, sometimes for months at a time. Their problems concern the platform, but their demands are broader. In a letter to Mark Zuckerberg, the most prominent philanthropic booster of the platform, the students as a collective write, "There is a huge class divide, with the children of the wealthy having small classes and real personalized learning in schools that minimize screen time, while public school students like us are expected to learn by a computer in front of our faces for hours at a time with educators only there to 'facilitate.'" After the brief media attention to this action subsides, Secondary School of Journalism is closed, replaced by a school focused on the creation of "cyberarts."

It is 2019. A group of organizers have successfully prevented the twin cities of Minneapolis–St. Paul from instituting a joint powers agreement which would allow data collected about students and their families by schools to be shared with other arms of government, including law enforcement, child welfare, and mental health services. In the eyes of these organizers, such data sharing amounts to surveillance and criminalization of youth, the construction of what they have dubbed "the cradle-to-prison algorithm"(Pfefferkorn, 2020). After successfully organizing to prevent the construction of this data pipeline, organizer Marika Pfefferkorn—cofounder of the Twin Cities Innovation Alliance and executive director of the Midwest Center for School Transformation—disputes the idea that government projects should first engage the communities they aim to serve. She is dissatisfied with the idea that technologists should merely consult with communities about tools and platforms they have already scoped, built, and deployed, relegating the input of community members to a meaningless stamp of approval. Pointing to the insufficiency of such measures, she says, "It's not just community engagement, it's the whole process, because community is a part of the entire process if we actually are talking about equity—and by my definition that means ownership and decision-making."

This book has brought together three aspects of datafication as it plays out in minoritized communities and the institutions that serve them: first, I looked at calls for access to technology and showed how such calls, even as they were hitched to all kinds of ethical reasoning and linked to desired policy outcomes, were modulated by different actors. Far from being some kind of exogenous motivator or shock to the system, digital technologies were quite easily adapted to existing forms of power and authority. In an "urban school" that serves Black and Latinx poor and working-class youth in South and East Los Angeles, different groups in the school and in the community made claims about what access to technology was supposed to do, and those claims gave them a certain legitimacy and reputational benefit. These benefits did not in any way depend on whether or not technology behaved the way it was supposed to. Perhaps more importantly, the use of digital technology was extractive, especially with respect to students and teachers: access to technology made real demands of money, time, labor, attention, and data.

Second, I looked at how a single urban school and a network of urban schools engaged with one obvious consequence of the greater use of various forms of digital technology in schools and in everyday life: more technology means more data. In addition, this proliferation of data leads to datalogical enframing, the process by all kinds of arguments, problems, values, and competing visions were reduced to operations of digital data. In almost every setting (including the ethnographic, multi-sited field work in this book) digital technologies of all kinds created mechanisms for authorities to surveil, sort, rank, aggregate, and predict via manipulation of data. This dynamic was especially stark in the school settings described, where use of specific hardware, software, apps, and platforms was mandatory. Students (and, to a lesser extent, teachers) were rarely free to make choices about whether or not they would use a particular tool or platform. School administrators, on the other hand, could demand the use of any tool or platform outright. Like other forms of power, the power to surveil and to meaningfully control the behavior of targeted subjects was unevenly distributed and accumulated more easily to parties with greater technological expertise. In the case of a charter management organization, busyness with the data generated by various forms of edtech conferred a reputational benefit on the whole organization. The use of tools and platforms common to the tech sector (data pipelines and dashboards) took the form of a demand for ever more data, but did not bestow any particular ability to use data to achieve desired ends.

Finally, I pointed to another part of datafication as it concerns a small but significant number of professional community organizers, people who are working to build grassroots political power in places where the state provides limited social welfare in favor of policing and other carceral policies. The organizers my research group is learning with and learning from are interested in data in two seemingly contradictory ways: first, these organizers are fighting the surveillance capacities of police and other authorities in their communities; and second, they are marshalling the capacities of digital data to their own movement-aligned political projects and to their own professional practice. In this way, these organizers recognize the trap of datalogical enframing, but they exert a form of what the Black Panther Party's revised Ten-Point Program might call "people's community control of technology."

In writing about minoritized communities and centering race in that analysis, I have tried to break out of moribund tropes about tech saviorism to instead point to more complex relations of technology and minoritized communities. The particular scholarly synthesis I have worked through in research and in writing this book do not lead to easy-to-swallow policy prescriptions about the best way to use technology or to structure the public sphere or to regulate the tech sector, although those are certainly all worthwhile endeavors. Instead, by way of conclusion, I point to three broad themes that run through this work and might lead to further questioning and analysis by other scholars, intellectuals, or community members.

Datafication as Cover for Racial Segregation

At the time of the writing of this book, a number of challenges to public education had spilled into public concern and national politics. First, the COVID-19 pandemic disrupted education for many students and families. Lockdowns and the institution of remote schooling spread many forms of unregulated edtech to homes and schools. Persistent reminders of this technical expression of inequality in public education impelled many advocates to argue that digital technologies were even more important to working-class students of color, the very logic of access to technology this book rebuts. Simultaneously, conservative legislators in a number of states seized on frustration over the condition of public education to offer novel legislation concerned with banning certain topics from schools, especially critical race theory. These efforts, immediately contested through legal action, constituted a right-wing political strategy that sought to gain advantage in national electoral politics by attacking the specific content of courses and the general terms by which public education is offered (Gabriel, 2023). Such measures variously sought to give control of curriculum to parents and/or professional politicians (as opposed to educators or administrators); to force schools to curtail the inclusion of trans students; to eliminate any mention of race, gender, or sexual orientation from U.S. history; and to outlaw any programmatic approach to diversity by a school or school system. While the success of these measures in their immediate goals or as a winning national electoral strategy remained dubious (although certainly possible), the simultaneous embrace of edtech and anti-democratic tactics by elected officials in the United States should immediately give the lie to the idea that access to technology might democratize, improve, or otherwise combat inequality in public education for working-class students of color or anyone else.

As harmful as such scapegoating might prove to be and as ineffective as further investment in edtech might turn out to be, these contemporary pressures on public education in the United States are an opportunity to revisit the goals and purpose of public education. Public education in the United States has always been an important political ambition and social cause for Black Americans: the public schooling of American children could be said to be rooted in the cause of Black freedom. The history of public education is, as Sojoyner (2016) writes it, about viable and practical alternatives to the plantation system, both in terms of disrupting its economic power via taxation and providing for the education (and presumed economic uplift) of poor and working-class peoples. Black freedom struggles have long focused on free, public education, including school desegregation and the formation of freedom schools, but this decades-long, concerted demand for provision of quality public education for all people in the United States has never been a reality. To the contrary, public schools in California and all over the United States have grown more racially segregated over the past thirty years.

A broad reevaluation of the civic purposes of urban schools must duly acknowledge the state's abdication of its duty to provide quality public education to minoritized communities. Given the extractions detailed in this book, the push to insert data-intensive edtech into urban schools can never contribute to racial justice or the development of a more educated, responsible citizenry. Revisiting the central argument of this book, the resource field denoted by the term *access to technology* cannot meaningfully contest the function of the racial project of segregated public education and, in fact, sits quite comfortably within it.

My primary admonition is this: the United States cannot use access to technology to ameliorate the racist status quo of racially segregated public education. There is no technological, computational, or datalogical answer for the racial segregation of U.S. schooling. As Kaba et al. (2021) write of technologies applied to policing, "Police violence won't end through technological advances (no matter what someone is selling you)" (p. 70). The same critique should be applied to edtech, which will not improve the results of segregated public education, despite the sensational claims of the tech sector. Only through collective action can any meaningful, lasting change occur. Spending on all kinds of edtech continues to rise without any evidence of its efficacy or even a passingly serious public conversation about what we want technology in schools to do. Claims of some general utility of digital technology to learning, as I have shown, are cynical, in that they distract from the persistent reality of racial segregation in U.S. public schooling and concentrate resources (primarily in the form of public funding) in the tech sector, a sector riven by racial hierarchies. Edtech accommodates the racial project of segregation and allows organizations to claim reputational benefits from working with digital data. The first move here has to be to dismiss out of hand the racial blamelessness of edtech. Race and public schooling, just like race and computing, are deeply, intimately related: in both arenas, racism is innovative.

But my admonition is not backward looking, because in the United States, there has never existed a nonhierarchical public life, no clear model we might use to rebuild or reformat public schooling (or any other shared undertaking) in Los Angeles or anywhere, no democratic project not already shaped by race, class, gender, sexuality, citizenship, and geography. Ferguson (2004) calls the citizen "a racialized emblem of heteronormativity whose universality exists at the expense of particularities of race, gender, and sexuality" (p. 12). In this read, the expense Ferguson is talking about is the domination of those marked by difference as compared to the unmarked, unraced, ungendered ideal of the citizen. Rosiek (2019) cites the critical race theorist Derrick Bell's concept of racial realism—a theory that echoes Du Bois's observations of the early twentieth century—to argue that racism is a more powerful force than public policy or data. A realist account would accept the innovative nature of racism, its ability to make itself over and take on new shapes. Recognizing that superficial policy changes would only shuffle students of color from one expression of institutional racism to another, he calls for a deeper, open-ended commitment to the well-being of students of color, not a task to be accomplished once and for all, but by successive and never-ceasing works of care by teachers and administrators working in solidarity with students and parents.

The racial realist approach would be to acknowledge the durability of racial segregation and other expressions of structural racism in the United States and to seek freedom in flight from those institutions. In different works, both Sojoyner (2013) and Gilmore (2017) point to the long tradition of marronage, an allusion to those enslaved persons who escaped the plantations of the Americas to form multiethnic exile communities of their own. This appeal to a fugitive sensibility speaks to the desire to build not just another world, but another kind of world, one that serves the particular needs of people of color, without the promise of persistence (Winston, 2023). Fugitive sensibility calls on us to build the spaces we need to escape, then let them evanesce or grow or transform according to their own norms and logics. There will certainly always be a need for such spaces, but is this our only hope for shared, public life?

Interpretation Matters

Throughout this text, I have attended to rhetorical, narrative, and affective dimensions of digital data, the way human activity exceeds and escapes its traces. Clearly, data-intensive forms of computation (including edtech) appeal because they make complex things like learning and schooling orderly and tractable. The ability of these technologies to meaningfully accomplish this action has been drastically misunderstood and deliberately obfuscated. The recent vogue for data-drivenness in public life relies on a faulty understanding of what data is and what it can do, one propped up by data's association with science and technology. Data promises us a way to know some external, independent, objective world, but that knowledge is a dangerous fantasy. Data-intensive computation is a powerful way of knowing, but there can be no single mode of representing the complexity of a world that is perpetually made and remade through the interaction and intra-action of knowledge production (Barad, 2007). This desire to know in a way that is durable and rises above conflict is, ironically, a source of dissensus in shared life and governance. Public life is a shared undertaking based on institutions, mutual interest, history, and culture: to pretend this project can be directed by data out there in the world, free of human judgment, is counterproductive, cynical, and undemocratic.

As Marres (2018) and others have argued, the desire for a durable basis of public life based on the bare facts of shared life is an enduring puzzle, one that is not resolved by contemporary technologies of knowing; instead, data-intensive computation proliferates knowledge claims and therefore, makes finding public facts more difficult, more complex. Facts are produced by authorities and based on social locations: the construction of immutable fact is a matter of interest for scholars, certainly, but as the response to public health measures taken in response to the COVID-19 pandemic have clearly shown, science and technology do not speak for themselves and cannot force the polity into order and reason.

Data and data-drivenness are tied up with a once glamorous, lucrative, and futuristic tech sector that has (through shrewd and unrelenting salesmanship) hovered outside the fray of a declining and sclerotic American empire, a post-industrial escape route from the persistence of industrial problems like urban schools. But whatever improvements the tech sector might confer, it metes out more stingily to minoritized peoples: the tech sector itself is riven by racism, and so also riven by the hierarchies of class, caste, sex, disability, and citizenship (Daniels, 2015; McGee, 2020).

With respect to digital data's role in public life, there are two things here, one simple, one difficult. First, for the simple part: the segregation of American schools (and the residential segregation that fuels it) belie any notion of racial progress in the Unites States. As Honig (2017) writes in a wonderfully evocative meditation on the relationship between artifacts and democracy,

> The public things of U.S. democracy have been part and parcel of a regime of white supremacy in which equal access to public things— accommodations, travel, parks, streets, wine trains, and more—are denied to people of color. In the context of white supremacy, public things have operated not to equalize people into citizenship but to communicate the terms of a differential citizenship and the frequently subordinating terms of governance and belonging. (p. 24)

Racial segregation changes over time, but the dominant classes of the nation have in no way committed to combatting the racial segregation that has been a feature of the United States since its foundation. Data cannot solve this problem. The second part concerns a difficult reimagining of what shared life can be in a racially segregated republic: scholars such as Dean Spade have denounced the nation-state as fundamentally unworkable, as contributing to the fundamental insecurity and precarity of contemporary life (Spade, 2020). Others have argued for nonhierarchical ways of building shared, public life, a move toward more recognizable democratic features of our past. In either case, we can be guided by Ferguson (2004), who argues that past intellectual and social movements such as Woman of Color Feminism direct us to see public life as "constructed, imaginative, and heterogenous, rather than as natural, objective, and homogeneous" (p. 117). It remains to be seen if any form of computation, data-intensive or otherwise, might aid in this imaginative project.

Studying Technology to Get Free

Technology-focused research—social scientific research that takes as its object the design, use, and consequences of digital technologies—has long been interested in the micro-politics of practice, how people sort out the constraints and affordances of technologies that increasingly mediate work, school, play, and everyday life. This research, carried out in a variety of fields, subfields, academic disciplines, and industry laboratories, is incredibly diverse and has, since at least the 1980s, provided important empirical exploration of what technology does in the world. But this research (including my own work), must contend with popular misconceptions and industry claims about what digital technology is. Research on technology, even when it disputes these ideas or argues against these specious claims, recapitulates the pleasant (and productive) fiction that digital technologies are ethically inert, that they are merely a means to achieve whatever end they have been assigned (Introna, 2006). Technology-focused research, despite (or perhaps, because of) its great heterogeneity has not been able to dislodge this idea. Even if, as Latour (2000) wrote decades ago, the assertion that technology and the social are mutually constituted is banal, that observation must still be reasserted today: digital technologies are part of the social world, which means they are also part of the racial world. They do not come from outside to produce "impacts," as in the mode of astronomical bodies: they are already here, in the world and of the world.

But digital technology has something to do with freedom, or, at least, it could. Alone, digital technologies are bland, inactive, blank, but the gag is that digital technologies are never alone. They are constantly animated and reanimated, invested with affective energy, productive force, and material agency. There are no computers in the wild, waiting to spring on the unwary. We make and remake the meaning of digital technology all the time, a meaning that is neither arbitrary, nor taken directly from the shape of an observer-independent universe. The meaning of digital computing is a discourse and a terrain of power, but like all forms of power it can never be complete or total. What if, instead of playing the mug's game of pursuing empirical research questions already deformed by the incredible claims of digital technology, research directed itself more seriously to the collective freedom of all peoples?

There are knowledge projects that can be formed in solidarity with emancipatory social movements, new multidisciplinarities that can be forged to address ongoing struggles, an endless array of scholarly objects that can be shaped to discover complex movements and actions. An interest in race is part of this action, but by no means its limit. Attention to power is called for, attention to the cut between public and private life, but this attention can also make room for joyfulness, exuberance, excess, love, lust, play, and reparation (Brock, 2019; Trammell, 2023). But as McKittrick (2021) reminds us, description is not liberation. I understand this to mean that descriptions of the lives of minoritized communities that only render them as bereft merely set the stage for further extraction, frequently executed under the guise of empowerment or paternalistic correction. Ferguson (2004) also points to this risk, writing of the sociological and literary enactments of Black abjection that amounted to representational enclosures which limited how Black people could exist in society without becoming unintelligible to others (and sadly, perhaps to themselves). These dynamics obtain for other minoritized peoples as well. The caution for researchers here is that well-intentioned descriptive research that merely rehearses expressions of the larger oppressions on their own do not necessarily resist, circumvent, or thwart those forces. Study is serious and can be seriously threatening, but it is not automatically so. As the organizers, students, parents, and teachers have shown throughout the years of my research, everywhere there is struggle, but everywhere people are boundless in their responses to what holds them down: creative, resourceful, joyful at turns; angry, self-serving, crafty at others.

Access is capture, but everywhere, people will find new ways to become free.

Notes

01. Access as Racial Progress

1. Much of the research on racial inequality and technology has used the terms *digital divide* or *digital inequality* to talk about access to technology, especially in the context of education. Rather than rehearse my objections to this framework in this book, I direct interested readers to my earlier work (Crooks, 2022).

2. *Racial capitalism* is an expansive term that has inspired a thriving and important community of research. However, I do not center my analysis on racial capitalism in the current work out of respect for the richness of that body of work, and due to an unwillingness to appropriate the work of authors who have cultivated those concepts. Readers who wish to explore this term should definitely refer to Cottom (2000), Johnson & Lubin (2017), and Robinson (2000).

3. As a super-talented computer science doctoral student who took one of my courses shared after we read and discussed Safiya Noble's book *Algorithms of Oppression* (2018), "As a computer scientist, this book angers me. And as a Black person, I am also sad that no one told me about it before."

4. As a reviewer of this book helpfully pointed out, there is a highly relevant strain of research in science and technology studies (STS) that takes up questions of publicness, democracy, and technology in all its manifestations. Given this book's focus, I have sidestepped much of this vital literature not out of indifference, but out of concern for space. See, for example, Latour & Weibel (2005), a collection that includes provocative works by many STS scholars who

think about how public life and democratic action are enacted or thwarted through technology.

5. I prefer the gender-inclusive term *Latinx* throughout this book, although the people I engaged with most often in my research used other terms to refer to themselves and others in their community, most often using the terms *Latino* or *Latina*.

6. In keeping with current popular usage and the way the term was used most frequently by research subjects, I treat the word *data* as a singular object (e.g., data *is*), as opposed to the more formal plural noun (e.g., data *are*).

7. A report on this field work was previously published; see Crooks (2019a).

8. Parts of this chapter were previously published; see Crooks (2019b) and Crooks (2021).

9. An abbreviated version of this empirical material was previously published; see Crooks (2017).

10. Part of this chapter was previously published; see Pei, Olgado, & Crooks (2022).

02. Access as Social Justice

1. There exists a successful multidisciplinary literature on education technology that incorporates critical approaches. Macgilchrist (2021) notes that critical approaches to the study of education technology draw widely from fields including education, sociology, media studies, history, and philosophy. The author describes this literature as pursuing three interests: transformation (i.e., the emergence of seemingly novel technologies and their societal implications); stability (i.e., the persistence of structural inequalities); and speculation (imaginative approaches that elicit imaginings of alternative ways of organizing the world). While I frequently cite many scholars who have contributed to critical studies of education technology, including foundational works by Larry Cuban, Audrey Watters, Neil Selwyn, Deborah Lupton, Carlo Perrotta, Ben Williamson, and others, I contrast my approach as being more interested in the experiences of minoritized communities than in education, which I treat as merely one mode of governance of public life.

2. Los Angeles media covered LAUSD's iPad program extensively. For a sample of the eventually negative reaction of journalists, teachers, and the

general public within the editorial pages of that paper, see Thornton (2014). For a summary of legal actions, including investigations by the Federal Bureau of Investigations and the Securities and Exchange Commission, see Keller (2014).

05. Access as Community Control

1. Later iterations of the workshop brought in Detroit Community Technology Project, Changing Frequencies, Twin Cities Innovation Alliance, and 8 to Abolition.

2. Safiya Noble (2018) reached this conclusion in her iconic book *Algorithms of Oppression* and repeated it in the pages of *Wired*: "An app will not save us. We will not sort out social inequality lying in bed staring at smartphones. It will not stem from simply sending emails to people in power, one person at a time."

3. This chapter synthesizes and extends my ongoing study of community organizers and their uses of data for movement work, including (Crooks, 2022, 2020; Pei & Crooks, 2023).

4. I take inspiration in this approach (and in many other aspects of scholarly and intellectual life) from Ruth Wilson Gilmore (Gilmore, 2007) , who shifts her focus in the final chapter of her classic *Golden Gulag* to demonstrate "the capacity of everyday people to organize and lead themselves" (185).

5. As one sign of the professionalization of community organizing, Harvard's Kennedy School offers a "15-week online executive program" called Leadership, Organizing and Action: Leading Change.

References

Alim, F., Cardozo, N., Gebhart, G., Gullo, K., & Kalia, A. (2017). Spying on students: School-issued devices and student privacy. *Electronic Frontier Foundation.* https://www.eff.org/files/2017/04/13/student-privacy-report .pdf

Alkebulan, P. (2007). *Survival pending revolution: The history of the Black Panther Party.* Tuscaloosa, AL: University of Alabama Press.

Allen, J. S. (2021). *There's a disco ball between us: A theory of black gay life.* Durham, NC: Duke University Press.

Ambrosio, J. (2013). Changing the subject: Neoliberalism and accountability in public education. *Educational Studies, 49*(4), 316–333. https://doi.org/10 .1080/00131946.2013.783835

Ames, M. G. (2016). Learning consumption: Media, literacy, and the legacy of One Laptop per Child. *The Information Society, 32*(2), 85–97. https://doi.org /10.1080/01972243.2016.1130497

Apple, M. W. (1995). *Education and power.* Abingdon-on-Thames, UK: Routledge.

Au, W. (2016). Meritocracy 2.0: High-stakes, standardized testing as a racial project of neoliberal multiculturalism. *Educational Policy, 30*(1), 39–62. https://doi.org/10.1177/0895904815614916

Au, W. (2021). Testing for whiteness? How high-stakes, standardized tests promote racism, undercut diversity, and undermine multicultural education. In H. P. Baptiste & J. Haynes Writer (Eds.), *Visioning multicultural education: Past, present, future* (pp. 1–15). Abingdon-on-Thames, UK: Routledge.

Bailey, M. (2021). *Misogynoir transformed: Black women's digital resistance.* New York, NY: New York University Press.

Barabas, C. (2022). Refusal in data ethics: Re-imagining the code beneath the code of computation in the carceral state. *Engaging Science, Technology, and Society,* 8(2), 1–23. https://doi.org/10.17351/ests2022.1233

Barad, K. (2007). *Meeting the universe halfway: Quantum physics and the entanglement of matter and meaning.* Durham, NC: Duke University Press Books.

Barlow, J. P. (1996). A declaration of the independence of cyberspace. The Electronic Frontier Foundation. https://www.eff.org/cyberspace -independence

Battle-Baptiste, W., & Rusert, B. (Eds.). (2018). *W. E. B Du Bois's data portraits: Visualizing Black America.* Amherst: The W. E. B. Du Bois Center at the University of Massachusetts; Princeton Architectural Press.

Baude, P., Casey, M., & Hanusheck, E. (2014). The evolution of charter school quality (NBER working paper no. 20645). National Bureau of Economic Research. www.nber.org/papers/w20645

Beer, D. (2017). The data analytics industry and the promises of real-time knowing: Perpetuating and deploying a rationality of speed. *Journal of Cultural Economy,* 10(1), 21–33. https://doi.org/10.1080/17530350.2016 .1230771

Benjamin, R. (2019). *Race after technology: Abolitionist tools for the new Jim code.* New York, NY: Polity.

Bickmore, D. L., & Sulentic Dowell, M-M. (2019). Understanding teacher turnover in two charter schools: Principal dispositions and practices. *International Journal of Leadership in Education,* 22(4), 387–405. https://doi .org/10.1080/13603124.2018.1481528

Bliss, C. (2013). The marketization of identity politics. *Sociology,* 47(5), 1011–1025. https://doi.org/10.1177/0038038513495604

Blume, H. (2013, September 25). Who pays if L.A. Unified students lose or break iPads? *Los Angeles Times.* http://articles.latimes.com/2013/sep/25 /local/la-me-ipads-lausd-20130926

Bonilla-Silva, E., & Dietrich, D. (2011). The sweet enchantment of color-blind racism in Obamerica. *The ANNALS of the American Academy of Political*

and *Social Science, 634*(1), 190–206. https://doi.org/10.1177/0002716210
389702

Borgman, C. L. (2015). *Big data, little data, no data: Scholarship in the networked world.* Cambridge, MA: MIT Press.

Bossewitch, J., & Sinnreich, A. (2013). The end of forgetting: Strategic agency beyond the panopticon. *New Media & Society, 15*(2), 224–242. https://doi.org/10.1177/1461444812451565

Boutte, G. S., & Johnson, G. L. Jr. (2013). Community and family involvement in urban schools. In H. R. Milner IV & K. Lomotey (Eds.), *Handbook of Urban Education* (pp. 167–186). Abingdon-on-Thames, UK: Routledge.

Bowen, W. G., Chingos, M. M., & McPherson, M. S. (2011). *Crossing the finish line: Completing college at America's public universities.* Princeton, NJ: Princeton University Press.

Bowker, G., Baker, K., Millerand, F., & Ribes, D. (2010). Towards information infrastructure Studies: Ways of knowing in a networked Environment. In J. Hunsinger, L. Klastrup, & M. Allen (Eds.), *International Handbook of Internet Research* (pp. 97–117). New York, NY: Springer. https://doi.org/10.1007/978-1-4020-9789-8_5

Bowker, G. C., & Star, S. L. (1999). *Sorting things out: Classification and its consequences.* Cambridge, MA: MIT Press.

Brock, A. L. (2019). *Distributed blackness: African American cybercultures.* New York, NY: New York University Press.

Brooks, E. (2020). Market-centered mania and network charter schools. In E. Brooks, *Education Reform in the Twenty-First Century* (pp. 1–27). London, UK: Palgrave Macmillan. https://doi.org/10.1007/978-3-030-61195-8_1

Browne, S. (2015). *Dark matters: On the surveillance of blackness.* Durham, NC: Duke University Press.

Buolamwini, J., & Gebru, T. (2018). Gender shades: Intersectional accuracy disparities in commercial gender classification. *Proceedings of Machine Learning Research, 81,* 77–91.

Buras, K. L. (2014). *Charter schools, race, and urban space: Where the market meets grassroots resistance.* Abingdon-on-Thames, UK: Routledge.

Buras, K. L., & Apple, M. W. (2005). School choice, neoliberal promises, and unpromising evidence. *Educational Policy, 19*(3), 550–564. https://doi.org/10.1177/0895904805276146

Burrell, J. (2016). How the machine 'thinks': Understanding opacity in machine learning algorithms. *Big Data & Society, 3*(1), 1–12. https://doi.org /10.1177/2053951715622512

Butler, J. (1996). An affirmative view. *Representations, 55*, 74–83.

California Department of Education. (2023). What are the Common Core Standards? https://www.cde.ca.gov/re/cc/whatareccss.asp

Christens, B. D., & Dolan, T. (2011). Interweaving youth development, community development, and social change through youth organizing. *Youth & Society, 43*(2), 528–548. https://doi.org/10.1177/0044118X10 383647

Christian, D., Lawrence, A., & Dampman, N. (2017). Increasing college access through the implementation of Naviance: An exploratory study. *Journal of College Access, 3*(2). http://scholarworks.wmich.edu/jca/vol3/iss2/4

Cifor, M., Garcia, P., Cowan, T. L., Rault, J., Sutherland, T., Chan, A., Rode, J., Hoffmann, A. L., Salehi, N., Nakamura, L. (2019). Feminist data manifest-no. https://www.manifestno.com/.

Cochran-Smith, M., Piazza, P., & Power, C. (2013). The politics of account-ability: Assessing teacher education in the United States. *The Educational Forum, 77*(1), 6–27. https://doi.org/10.1080/00131725.2013.739015

Coleman, B. (2009). Race as technology. *Camera Obscura: Feminism, Culture, and Media Studies, 24*(1), 177–207. https://doi.org/10.1215/02705346 -2008-018

Coleman, G. (2017). From internet farming to weapons of the geek. *Current Anthropology, 58*(Supplement 15), S91–S102.

The Combahee River Collective. (1977, 2014). A Black feminist statement. *Women's Studies Quarterly, 42*(3/4), 271–280.

Cope, B., & Kalantzis, M. (2016). Big Data comes to school: Implications for learning, assessment, and research. *AERA Open, 2*(2). https://doi.org/10 .1177/2332858416641907

Crooks, R. (2017). Representationalism at work: Dashboards and data analytics in urban education. *Educational Media International, 54*(4), 289–303. https://doi.org/10.1080/09523987.2017.1408267

Crooks, R. (2019a). Times thirty: Access, maintenance, and justice. *Science, Technology, & Human Values, 44*(1), 118–142. https://doi.org/10.1177 /0162243918783053

Crooks, R. (2019b). Cat-and-mouse games: Dataveillance and performativity in urban schools. *Surveillance & Society*, 17(3/4), 484–498. https://doi.org/10.24908/ss.v17i3/4.7098

Crooks, R. (2020, October). Between communication and violence. *ACM Interactions*, 27(5), 60–65.

Crooks, R. (2021). Productive myopia: Racialized organizations and edtech. *Big Data & Society*, 8(2), 1–16. https://doi.org/10.1177/20539517211050499

Crooks, R. (2022). Toward people's community control of technology: Race, access, and education. Social Science Research Council. https://doi.org/10.35650/JT.3015.d.2022

Crooks, R. (2022a). Seeking liberation: Surveillance, datafication, and race. *Surveillance & Society*, 20(4), 413–419. https://doi.org/10.24908/ss.v20i4.15983

Crooks, R., & Currie, M. (2021). Numbers will not save us: Agonistic data practices. *The Information Society*, 37(4),1–19. https://doi.org/10.1080/01972243.2021.1920081

Cuban, L. (2003). *Oversold and underused: Computers in the classroom.* Cambridge, MA: Harvard University Press.

Daniels, J. (2015). "My brain database doesn't see skin color": Color-blind racism in the technology industry and in theorizing the web. *American Behavioral Scientist*, 59(11), 1377–1393. https://doi.org/10.1177/0002764215578728

Data 4 Black Lives. (n.d.). https://d4bl.org.

Datafication and Community Activism Workshop. (2019, March 22) What we mean when we say #AbolishBigData2019. *Medium.* https://medium.com/@rncrooks/what-we-mean-when-we-say-abolishbigdata2019-d030799ab22e

Davis, L. P., & Museus, S. D. (2019). What is deficit thinking? An analysis of conceptualizations of deficit thinking and implications for scholarly research. *NCID Currents*, 1(1). https://doi.org/10.3998/currents.17387731.0001.110

Day, R. E. (2011). Death of the user: Reconceptualizing subjects, objects, and their relations. *Journal of the American Society for Information Science and Technology*, 62(1), 78–88. https://doi.org/10.1002/asi.21422

de Bastion. G., & Mukku, S. (2020). Data and the Global South: Key issues for inclusive digital development [White paper]. Heinrich Böll Foundation. https://us.boell.org/en/2020/10/20/data-and-global-south-key-issues-inclusive-digital-development

Dencik, L., Hintz, A., Redden, J., & Treré, E. (2022). *Data justice*. Thousand Oaks, CA: Sage Publications.

D'Ignazio, C., & Klein, L. F. (2023). *Data feminism*. Cambridge, MA: MIT Press.

Dishon, G., & Goodman, J. F. (2017). No-excuses for character: A critique of character education in no-excuses charter schools. *Theory and Research in Education*, *15*(2), 182–201. https://doi.org/10.1177/1477878517720162

Dourish, P. (2016). Algorithms and their others: Algorithmic culture in context. *Big Data & Society*, *3*(2), 1–11. https://doi.org/10.1177/2053951716665128

Dourish, P., & Gómez Cruz, E. (2018). Datafication and data fiction: Narrating data and narrating with data. *Big Data & Society*, *5*(2), 1–10. https://doi.org/10.1177/2053951718784083

Drucker, J. (2014). *Graphesis: Visual forms of knowledge production*. Cambridge, MA: Harvard University Press.

Egalite, A. J., Fusarelli, L. D., & Fusarelli, B. C. (2017). Will decentralization affect educational inequity? The Every Student Succeeds Act. *Educational Administration Quarterly*, *53*(5), 757–781. https://doi.org/10.1177/0013161X17735869

Erickson, A. T. (2016). *Making the unequal metropolis: School desegregation and its limits*. Chicago, IL: University of Chicago Press.

Eubanks, V. (2011). *Digital dead end: Fighting for social justice in the information age*. Cambridge, MA: MIT Press.

Eubanks, V. (2017). *Automating inequality: How high-tech tools profile, police, and punish the poor*. New York, NY: St. Martin's Press.

Farman, J. (2012). *Mobile interface theory: Embodied space and locative media*. Abingdon-on-Thames, UK: Routledge.

Farman, J. (2017). Repair and software: Updates, obsolescence, and mobile culture's operating systems. *Continent*, *6*(1), 20–24.

Ferguson, R. A. (2004). *Aberrations in black: Toward a queer of color critique*. Minneapolis, MN: University of Minnesota Press.

Ferguson, R. A. (2012). *The reorder of things: The university and its pedagogies of minority difference*. Minneapolis, MN: University of Minnesota Press.

Ferguson, R. A. (2020). Race. In B. Burgett & G. Hendler (Eds.), *Keywords for American cultural studies* (3rd ed., pp. 207–211). New York, NY: New York University Press.

Few, S. (2006). *Information dashboard design: The effective visual communication of data.* Sebastopol, CA: O'Reilly Media.

Fine, M., Freudenberg, N., Payne, Y., Perkins, T., Smith, K., & Wanzer, K. (2003). "Anything can happen with police around": Urban youth evaluate strategies of surveillance in public places. *Journal of Social Issues, 59*(1), 141–158. https://doi.org/10.1111/1540-4560.t01-1-00009

Fisher-Ari, T., Kavanagh, K., & Martin, A. (2016). Urban teachers struggling within and against neoliberal, accountability-era policies. *Perspectives on Urban Education, 13*(2), 1–18.

Frankenberg, E., Siegel-Hawley, G., Wang, J., & Orfield, G. (2010). Choice without equity: Charter school segregation and the need for civil rights standards. The Civil Rights Project at UCLA. http://escholarship.org/uc/item/4r07q8kg

Fricchione, M. J., Seo, J. Y., & Arwady, M. A. (2021). Data-driven reopening of urban public education through Chicago's tracking of COVID-19 school transmission. *Journal of Public Health Management and Practice, 27*(3), 229–232. https://doi.org/10.1097/PHH.0000000000001334

Gabriel, T. (2023, February 6). Education issues vault to top of the G.O.P.'s presidential race. *The New York Times.* https://www.nytimes.com/2023/02/06/us/politics/education-republicans-elections.html

Ganesh, S. (2016). Managing surveillance: Surveillant individualism in an era of relentless visibility. *International Journal of Communication, 10*(0), 14.

Garcia, A., & Morrell, E. (2013). City youth and the pedagogy of participatory media. *Learning, Media and Technology, 38*(2), 123–127. https://doi.org/10.1080/17439884.2013.782040

Gawlik, M. (2012). Moving beyond the rhetoric: Charter school reform and accountability. *The Journal of Educational Research, 105*(3), 210–219. https://doi.org/DOI:10.1080/00220671.2011.559492

Gillborn, D., Warmington, P., & Demack, S. (2018). QuantCrit: Education, policy, "Big Data" and principles for a critical race theory of statistics. *Race Ethnicity and Education, 21*(2), 158–179. https://doi.org/10.1080/13613324.2017.1377417

Gilliom, J. (2006). Struggling with surveillance: Resistance, consciousness, and identity. In R. V. Ericson & K. D. Haggerty (Eds.), *The New Politics of Surveillance and Visibility* (pp. 111–129). Toronto, ON: University of Toronto Press.

Gilliom, J. (2010). Lying, cheating and teaching to the test: The politics of surveillance under No Child Left Behind. In T. Monahan & R. D. Torres (Eds.), *Schools under surveillance: Cultures of control in public education* (pp. 194–209). New Brunswick, NJ: Rutgers University Press.

Gilliom, J., & Monahan, T. (2012). *SuperVision: An introduction to the surveillance society.* Chicago, IL: University of Chicago Press.

Gilmore, R. W. (2007). *Golden gulag: Prisons, surplus, crisis, and opposition in globalizing California.* Berkeley, CA: University of California Press.

Gilmore, R. W. (2017). Abolition geography and the problem of innocence. In G. T. Johnson & A. Lubin (Eds.), *Futures of Black radicalism* (pp. 225–240). London, UK: Verso.

Gitelman, L. (Ed.). (2013). *"Raw data" is an oxymoron.* Cambridge, MA: MIT Press.

Gitelman, L. (2014). *Paper knowledge: Toward a media history of documents.* Durham, NC: Duke University Press.

Good, K. D. (2020). *Bring the world to the child: Technologies of global citizenship in American education.* Cambridge, MA: MIT Press.

Gordon, A. (2017). The bruise blues. In G. T. Johnson & A. Lubin (Eds.), *Futures of Black radicalism* (pp. 194–205). London, UK: Verso.

Gray, J. (2018). Three aspects of data worlds. *Krisis: Journal for Contemporary Philosophy, 1,* 4–17.

Greene, D. (2021). *The promise of access: Technology, inequality, and the political economy of hope.* Cambridge, MA: MIT Press.

Haggerty, K., & Ericson, R. (2000). The surveillant assemblage. *British Journal of Sociology, 51*(4), 605–622.

Harmon, N. (2012). The role of minority-serving institutions in national college completion goals. Institute for Higher Education Policy. https://eric.ed.gov/?id=ED528603

Harris, C. P. (2023). To build a black future: The radical politics of joy, pain, and care. Princeton, NJ: Princeton University Press.

Heaven, W. D. (2020, July 17). Predictive policing algorithms are racist. They need to be dismantled. *MIT Technology Review.* https://www.technology

review.com/2020/07/17/1005396/predictive-policing-algorithms-racist -dismantled-machine-learning-bias-criminal-justice/

Heeks, R., & Shekhar, S. (2019). Datafication, development and marginalised urban communities: An applied data justice framework. *Information, Communication & Society, 22*(7), 992–1011. https://doi.org/10.1080 /1369118X.2019.1599039

Holbein, J. B., & Ladd, H. F. (2017). Accountability pressure: Regression discontinuity estimates of how No Child Left Behind influenced student behavior. *Economics of Education Review, 58*, 55–67. https://doi.org/10.1016 /j.econedurev.2017.03.005

Honig, B. (2017). *Public things: Democracy in disrepair.* New York, NY: Fordham University Press.

Introna, L. D. (2006). Maintaining the reversibility of foldings: Making the ethics (politics) of information technology visible. *Ethics and Information Technology, 9*(1), 11–25. https://doi.org/10.1007/s10676-006-9133-z

Jarke, J., & Breiter, A. (2019). Editorial: The datafication of education. *Learning, Media and Technology, 44*(1), 1–6. https://doi.org/10.1080 /17439884.2019.1573833

Jenkins, K. (2014). "That's not philosophy": Feminism, academia and the double bind. *Journal of Gender Studies, 23*(3), 262–274. https://doi.org/10 .1080/09589236.2014.909720

Johnson, G. T., & Lubin, A. (Eds.). (2017). *Futures of Black radicalism.* London, UK: Verso.

Kaba, M., Murakawa, N., & Nopper, T. K. (2021). *We do this 'til we free us: Abolitionist organizing and transforming justice.* Chicago, IL: Haymarket Books.

Keaton, T. (2018). Race. In E. R. Edwards, R. A. Ferguson, & J. O. G. Ogbar (Eds.), *Keywords for African American studies* (pp. 163–167). New York, NY: New York University Press. https://www.degruyter.com/isbn/97814798 10253

Kelly, A. E. (2017). Is learning data in the right shape? *Journal of Learning Analytics, 4*(2), 154–159.

Kennedy, H., & Hill, R. L. (2016). The pleasure and pain of visualizing data in times of data power. *Television and New Media, 18*(8),1–14. https://doi.org /10.1177/1527476416667823

King, J. L. (2004). Rob Kling and the Irvine School. *The Information Society, 20*(2), 97–99. https://doi.org/10.1080/01972240490422978

King, M., Rothberg, S., Dawson, R., & Batmaz, F. (2016). Bridging the edtech evidence gap: A realist evaluation framework refined for complex technology initiatives. *Journal of Systems and Information Technology, 18*(1), 18–40. https://doi.org/10.1108/JSIT-06-2015-0059

Kling, R. (1991). Computerization and social transformations. *Science, Technology, & Human Values, 16*(3), 342–367. https://doi.org/10.1177/0162 24399101600304

Knaus, C. B. (2014). Seeing what they want to see: Racism and leadership development in urban schools. *The Urban Review, 46*(3), 420–444. https://doi.org/10.1007/s11256-014-0299-0

Knox, J., Williamson, B., & Bayne, S. (2019). Machine behaviourism: Future visions of "learnification" and "datafication" across humans and digital technologies. *Learning, Media and Technology, 45*(1), 1–15. https://doi.org /10.1080/17439884.2019.1623251

Kohli, S., Resmovits, J., & Knoll, C. (2016, November 10). Thousands of L.A. County high school students stage walkouts to protest Donald Trump's victory. *The Los Angeles Times.* https://www.latimes.com/local/california /la-me-ln-high-school-walkout-trump-20161110-story.html

Korhonen, V. (2024, March 6). E-learning and digital education: Statistics & facts. *Statista.* https://www.statista.com/topics/3115/e-learning-and -digital-education/#topicOverview

Kupchik, A., & Ward, G. (2014). Race, poverty, and exclusionary school security: An empirical analysis of U.S. elementary, middle, and high schools. *Youth Violence and Juvenile Justice, 12*(4), 332–354. https://doi.org /10.1177/1541204013503890

Lack, B. (2009). No excuses: A critique of the Knowledge Is Power Program (KIPP) within charter schools in the USA. *Journal for Critical Education Policy Studies, 7*(2), 127–152.

Latour, B. (2000). The Berlin key or how to do words with things. In P. Graves-Brown (Ed.), *Matter, materiality, and modern culture* (pp. 10–21). Oxfordshire, UK: Routledge.

Latour, B. (2013). *An inquiry into modes of existence: An anthropology of the moderns* (C. Porter, Trans.). Cambridge, MA: Harvard University Press.

Latour, B., & Weibel, P. (Eds.). (2005). *Making things public: Atmospheres of democracy.* Cambridge, MA: MIT Press.

Lauen, D. L., Fuller, B., & Dauter, L. (2015). Positioning charter schools in Los Angeles: Diversity of form and homogeneity of effects. *American Journal of Education, 121*(2), 213–239. https://doi.org/10.1086/679391

Lenhoff, S. W., & Pogodzinski, B. (2018). School organizational effectiveness and chronic absenteeism: Implications for accountability. *Journal of Education for Students Placed at Risk (JESPAR), 23*(1–2), 153–169. https://doi.org/10.1080/10824669.2018.1434656

Licklider, J. C. R. (1960). Man-computer symbiosis. *IRE Transactions on Human Factors in Electronics, HFE* (1), 4–11.

Los Angeles Times Data Desk. (2009). South Park profile. *Los Angeles Times.* http://maps.latimes.com/neighborhoods/neighborhood/south-park/

Losen, D., Goyal, S., Alam, M., & Salazar, R. (2022). Unmasking school discipline disparities in California: What the 2019–2020 data can tell us about problems and progress. Center for Civil Rights Remedies at UCLA's Civil Rights Project. https://www.civilrightsproject.ucla.edu/resources/projects/center-for-civil-rights-remedies/school-to-prison-folder/summary-reports/unmasking-school-discipline-disparities-in-california/Unmasking_School_Disclipline_Disparities_CA_Report.pdf

Macgilchrist, F. (2021). What is "critical" in critical studies of edtech? Three responses. *Learning, Media and Technology, 46*(3), 243–249. https://doi.org/10.1080/17439884.2021.1958843

Margolin, J., Heppen, J., Haynes, E., Ruedel, K., Meakin, J., Rickles, J., Samkian, A., O'Brien, B., Surr, W., & Fellers, L. (2015). Evaluation of LAUSD's instructional technology initiative. American Institutes for Research.

Marres, N. (2018). Why we can't have our facts back. *Engaging Science, Technology, and Society, 4,* 423–433. https://doi.org/10.17351/ests2018.188

Martin, N. D., Spenner, K. I., & Mustillo, S. A. (2017). A test of leading explanations for the college racial-ethnic achievement gap: Evidence from a longitudinal case study. *Research in Higher Education, 58*(6), 617–645. https://doi.org/10.1007/s11162-016-9439-6

Martinez HoSang, D., & LaBennett, O. (2020). Racialization. In B. Burgett & G. Hendler (Eds.), *Keywords for American cultural studies* (3rd ed., pp. 212–214). New York University Press.

Mazmanian, M., & Beckman, C. M. (2018). "Making" your numbers: Engendering organizational control through a ritual of quantification. *Organization Science, 29*(3), 357–379. https://doi.org/10.1287/orsc.2017.1185

McGee, E. O. (2020). Interrogating structural racism in STEM higher education. *Educational Researcher, 49*(9), 633–644. https://doi.org/10.3102/0013189X20972718

McGranahan, C. (2016). Theorizing refusal: An introduction. *Cultural Anthropology, 31*(3), 319–325. https://doi.org/10.14506/ca31.3.01

McKittrick, K. (2021). *Dear science and other stories.* Durham, NC: Duke University Press.

McMillan Cottom, T. (2020). Where platform capitalism and racial capitalism meet: The sociology of race and racism in the digital society. *Sociology of Race and Ethnicity, 6*(4), 441–449. https://doi.org/10.1177/2332649220949473

Means, A. (2013). *Schooling in the age of austerity: Urban education and the struggle for democratic life.* New York, NY: Springer.

Medina Falzone, G. (2022). Case studies in social death: The criminalization and dehumanization of six Black and Latino boys. *The Urban Review, 54*(2), 233–254. https://doi.org/10.1007/s11256-021-00617-y

Meiners, E. R. (2011). Ending the school-to-prison pipeline/Building abolition futures. *The Urban Review, 43*(4), 547–565. https://doi.org/10.1007/s11256-011-0187-9

Mijs, J. J. B. (2016). The unfulfillable promise of meritocracy: Three lessons and their implications for justice in education. *Social Justice Research, 29*(1), 14–34. https://doi.org/10.1007/s11211-014-0228-0

Milan, S., & van der Velden, L. (2016). The alternative epistemologies of data activism. *Digital Culture & Society, 2*(2), 57–74. https://doi.org/10.14361/dcs-2016-0205

Mirón, L., & St. John, E. (Eds.). (2003). *Reinterpreting urban school reform: Have urban schools failed, or has the reform movement failed urban schools?* Albany, NY: State University of New York Press.

Monahan, T. (2008). Picturing technological change: The materiality of information infrastructures in public education. *Technology, Pedagogy and Education, 17*(2), 89–101. https://doi.org/10.1080/14759390802098581

Monahan, T. (2011). Surveillance as cultural practice. *The Sociological Quarterly*, 52(4), 495–508.

Monahan, T., & Torres, R. D. (Eds.). (2010). *Schools under surveillance: Cultures of control in public education*. New Brunswick, NJ: Rutgers University Press.

Mountz, S. (2020). Remapping pipelines and pathways: Listening to queer and transgender youth of color's trajectories through girls' juvenile justice facilities. *Affilia*, 35(2), 177–199. https://doi.org/10.1177/0886109919880517

Muhammad, K. G. (2010). *The condemnation of blackness: Race, crime, and the making of modern urban America*. Cambridge, MA: Harvard University Press

Muñoz, J. E. (1999). *Disidentifications: Queers of color and the performance of politics*. Minneapolis, MN: University of Minnesota Press.

Murnane, R., & Cohen, D. (1986). Merit pay and the evaluation problem: Why most merit pay plans fail and a few survive. *Harvard Educational Review*, 56(1), 1–18. https://doi.org/10.17763/haer.56.1.l8q2334243271116

Nakamura, L., & Chow-White, P. (Eds.). (2012). *Race after the internet*. Abingdon-on-Thames, UK: Routledge.

Nanda, J. (2019). The construction and criminalization of disability in school incarceration. *Columbia Journal of Race and Law*, 9(2). https://heinonline .org/HOL/P?h=hein.journals/cjoral9&i=265

Narayan, J. (2020). Survival pending revolution: Self-determination in the age of proto-neo-liberal globalization. *Current Sociology*, 68(2), 187–203. https://doi.org/10.1177/0011392119886870

Neff, G., Tanweer, A., Fiore-Gartland, B., & Osburn, L. (2017). Critique and contribute: A practice-based framework for improving critical data studies and data science. *Big Data*, 5(2), 85–97. https://doi.org/10.1089 /big.2016.0050

Nelson, A. (2011). *Body and soul: The Black Panther Party and the fight against medical discrimination*. Minneapolis, MN: University of Minnesota Press.

Nelson, A. (2016). *The social life of DNA: Race, reparations, and reconciliation after the genome*. Boston, MA: Beacon Press.

Nelson, A., Tu, T. L. N., & Headlam Hines, A. (Eds.). (2001). *Technicolor: Race, technology, and everyday life*. New York, NY: New York University Press.

Nemorin, S. (2017). Post-panoptic pedagogies: The changing nature of school surveillance in the digital age. *Surveillance & Society*, *15*(2), 239–253.

Noble, S. U. (2016). A future for intersectional Black feminist technology studies. *S&F Online*, *13*(3). http://sfonline.barnard.edu/traversing-technologies/safiya-umoja-noble-a-future-for-intersectional-black-feminist-technology-studies/

Noble, S. U. (2018). *Algorithms of oppression: How search engines reinforce racism*. New York, NY: New York University Press.

Noble, S. U. (2018, March 4). Social inequality will not be solved by an app. *Wired*. https://www.wired.com/story/social-inequality-will-not-be-solved-by-an-app/

Noble, S. U., & Tynes, B. M. (Eds.). (2015). *The intersectional internet: Race, sex, class and culture online*. Lausanne, Switzerland: Peter Lang Publishing.

Omi, M., & Winant, H. (2016). Racial formation in the United States. In W. Longhofer & D. Winchester (Eds.), *Social theory re-wired: New connections to classical and contemporary perspectives* (pp. 378–393). London, UK: Taylor & Francis Group. https://public.ebookcentral.proquest.com/choice/publicfullrecord.aspx?p=4470185

Orfield, G., & Ee, J. (2014). *Segregating California's future: Inequality and its alternative 60 years after Brown v. Board of Education*. The Civil Rights Project at UCLA. https://www.civilrightsproject.ucla.edu/research/k-12-education/integration-and-diversity/segregating-california2019s-future-inequality-and-its-alternative-60-years-after-brown-v.-board-of-education

Orfield, G., Ee, J., Frankenberg, E., & Siegel-Hawley, G. (2016). *Brown at 62: School segregation by race, poverty and state*. The Civil Rights Project at UCLA. https://escholarship.org/uc/item/5ds6kord#author

Orfield, G., Erica, F., Ee, J., & Jennifer, A. (2019). *Harming our common future: America's segregated schools 65 years after Brown*. The Civil Rights Project at UCLA. escholarship.org/uc/item/23j1b9nv

Orfield, G., & Jarvie, D. (2020). *Black segregation matters: School resegregation and Black educational opportunity*. The Civil Rights Project at UCLA. https://eric.ed.gov/?id=ED610039

Palardy, G., Rumberger, R., & Butler, T. (2015). The effect of high school socioeconomic, racial, and linguistic segregation on academic performance and school behaviors. *Teachers College Record*, *117*(12), 1–52.

Passi, S., & Jackson, S. (2017). Data vision: Learning to see through algorithmic abstraction. *Proceedings of the 2017 ACM Conference on Computer Supported Cooperative Work and Social Computing*, 2436–2447. https://doi.org/10.1145/2998181.2998331

Pearman, F. A., & Swain, W. A. (2017). School choice, gentrification, and the variable significance of racial stratification in urban neighborhoods. *Sociology of Education, 90*(3), 1–24. https://doi.org/10.1177/0038040717710494

Pei, L., Olgado, B. S., & Crooks, R. (2022). Narrativity, audience, legitimacy: Data practices of community organizers. *CHI Conference on Human Factors in Computing Systems Extended Abstracts*, 1–6. https://doi.org/10.1145/3491101.3519673

Penuel, W. R. (2006). Implementation and effects of one-to-one computing initiatives: A research synthesis. *Journal of Research on Technology in Education, 38*(3), 329–348. https://doi.org/10.1080/15391523.2006.10782463

Perrotta, C., & Williamson, B. (2018). The social life of learning analytics: Cluster analysis and the 'performance' of algorithmic education. *Learning, Media and Technology, 43*(1), 3–16. https://doi.org/10.1080/17439884.2016.1182927

Pfefferkorn, Marika. (2020, December 14). Oral histories of surveillance. Interview by Lexi Spencer-Notabartolo. Our Data Bodies Oral Histories Series. https://www.odbproject.org/2020/12/14/marika-pfefferkorn-oral-histories-of-surveillance/

Pham, L. D., Nguyen, T. D., & Springer, M. G. (2021). Teacher merit pay: A meta-analysis. *American Educational Research Journal, 58*(3), 527–566. https://doi.org/10.3102/0002831220905580

Pickert, K. (2014, October 17). How the iPad helped bring down the Los Angeles schools chief. *Time.* https://time.com/3514155/ipad-john-deasy-lausd-superintendent-resigns/

Pierre, J., Crooks, R., Currie, M., Paris, B., & Pasquetto, I. (2021). Getting ourselves together: Data-centered participatory design research and epistemic burden. *Proceedings of the 2021 CHI Conference on Human Factors in Computing Systems*, 1–11. https://doi.org/10.1145/3411764.3445103

Porter, T. M. (1996). *Trust in numbers: The pursuit of objectivity in science and public life.* Princeton, NJ: Princeton University Press.

Raible, J., & Irizarry, J. G. (2010). Redirecting the teacher's gaze: Teacher education, youth surveillance and the school-to-prison pipeline. *Teaching and Teacher Education, 26*(5), 1196–1203. https://doi.org/10.1016/j.tate.2010.02.006

Rasheed, R. A., Kamsin, A., & Abdullah, N. A. (2020). Challenges in the online component of blended learning: A systematic review. *Computers & Education, 144*, 1–17. https://doi.org/10.1016/j.compedu.2019.103701

Ray, V. (2019). A Theory of racialized organizations. *American Sociological Review, 84*(1), 26–53. https://doi.org/10.1177/0003122418822335

Richardson, A. V. (2020). *Bearing witness while black: African Americans, smartphones, and the new protest #Journalism.* Oxford, UK: Oxford University Press.

Robinson, C. J. (2000). *Black Marxism: The making of the Black radical tradition.* Chapel Hill. NC: University of North Carolina Press.

Rosiek, J. (2019). School segregation: A realist's view. *Phi Delta Kappan, 100*(5), 8–13. https://doi.org/10.1177/0031721719827536

Sadowski, J. (2019). When data is capital: Datafication, accumulation, and extraction. *Big Data & Society, 6*(1), 1–12. https://doi.org/10.1177/2053951718820549

Schüll, N. D. (2014). *Addiction by design: Machine gambling in Las Vegas.* Princeton, NJ: Princeton University Press.

Schutt, R., & O'Neil, C. (2013). *Doing data science: Straight talk from the frontline.* Sebastopol, CA: O'Reilly Media.

Scott, J. C. (1998). *Seeing like a state: How certain schemes to improve the human condition have failed.* New Haven, CT: Yale University Press.

Seaver, N. (2017). Algorithms as culture: Some tactics for the ethnography of algorithmic systems. *Big Data & Society, 4*(2), 1–12. https://doi.org/10.1177/2053951717738104

Selwyn, N. (2016). 'There's so much data': Exploring the realities of data-based school governance. *European Educational Research Journal, 15*(1), 54–68. https://doi.org/10.1177/1474904115602909

Sharma, M. (2018). Seeping deficit thinking assumptions maintain the neoliberal education agenda: Exploring three conceptual frameworks of deficit thinking in inner-city schools. *Education and Urban Society, 50*(2), 136–154. https://doi.org/10.1177/0013124516682301

Simmons, L. (2017). *The prison school: Educational inequality and school discipline in the age of mass incarceration*. Oakland, CA: University of California Press.

Simpson, A. (2007). On ethnographic refusal: Indigeneity, 'voice' and colonial citizenship. *Junctures, 9*, 66–80.

Sims, C. (2017). *Disruptive fixation: School reform and the pitfalls of techno-idealism*. Princeton, NJ: Princeton University Press.

Slade, S., & Prinsloo, P. (2013). Learning analytics: Ethical issues and dilemmas. *American Behavioral Scientist, 57*(10), 1510–1529. https://doi.org/10.1177/0002764213479366

Sojoyner, D., M. (2013). Black radicals make for bad citizens: Undoing the myth of the school to prison pipeline. *Berkeley Review of Education 4* (2), 241–263. https://doi.org/10.5070/B84110021

Sojoyner, D. M. (2016). *First strike: Educational enclosures in Black Los Angeles*. Minneapolis, MN: University of Minnesota Press.

Spade, D. (2020). Solidarity not charity. *Social Text, 38* (1), 131–151. https://doi.org/10.1215/01642472-7971139

Stalder, F. (2002). Failures and successes: Notes on the development of electronic cash. *The Information Society, 18*(3), 209–219. https://doi.org/10.1080/01972240290074968

Stassen, M. (2012). Accountable for what? *Journal of Assessment and Institutional Effectiveness, 2*(2), 137–142.

Stokes, K. (2018, August 29). Why LAUSD's 30,000 teachers have gone on strike. *LAist*. https://laist.com/news/why-lausds-30000-teachers-might-go-on-strike

Stop LAPD Spying Coalition, & Free Radicals. (2020, March 2). The algorithmic ecology: An abolitionist tool for organizing against algorithms. *Medium*. https://medium.com/@stoplapdspying/the-algorithmic-ecology-an-abolitionist-tool-for-organizing-against-algorithms-14fcbd0e64d0

Suchman, L. (1996). Supporting articulation work. In R. Kling (Ed.), *Computerization and controversy: Value conflicts and social choices* (2nd ed.). Burlington, MA: Morgan Kaufmann.

Taylor, E. (2013). *Surveillance schools: Security, discipline and control in contemporary education*. New York, NY: Springer.

Thompson, G., & Cook, I. (2013). Mapping teacher-faces. *Studies in Philosophy and Education, 32*(4), 379–395. https://doi.org/10.1007/s11217-012-9335-2

Thornton, P. (2014, January 4). No end to LAUSD iPad debate. *The Los Angeles Times*. https://www.latimes.com/opinion/la-xpm-2014-jan-04-la-le-0104-lausd-ipad-mailbag-20140104-story.html

Trammell, A. (2023). *Repairing play: A Black phenomenology*. Cambridge, MA: MIT Press.

Vertesi, J., & Dourish, P. (2011). The value of data: Considering the context of production in data economies. *CSCW '11: Proceedings of the ACM 2011 Conference on Computer-Supported Cooperative Work*, 533–542. https://doi.org/10.1145/1958824.1958906.

Vinson, K., & Ross, E. W. (2000). Education and the new disciplinarity: Surveillance, spectacle, and the case of SBER. *Cultural Logic, 4*(1). https://ojs.library.ubc.ca/index.php/clogic/article/view/191988/188923

Wan, T. (2021, 20). Hobsons' higher ed business split and sold in separate deals totaling $410M. *Ed Surge*. https://www.edsurge.com/news/2021-02-20-hobsons-higher-ed-business-split-and-sold-in-separate-deals-totaling-410m

Warschauer, M., & Matuchniak, T. (2010). New technology and digital worlds: Analyzing evidence of equity in access, use, and outcomes. *Review of Research in Education, 34*(1), 179–225. https://doi.org/10.3102/0091732X09349791

Whitman, M. (2020). "We called that a behavior": The making of institutional data. *Big Data & Society, 7*(1), 205395172093220. https://doi.org/10.1177/2053951720932200

Williamson, B. (2017). Calculating children in the dataveillance school: Personal and learning analytics. In E. Taylor & T. Rooney (Eds.), *Surveillance futures: Social and ethical implications of new technologies for children and young people* (pp. 50–65). Abingdon-on-Thames, UK: Routledge.

Winston, B. (2007). Let them eat laptops: The limits of technicism. *International Journal of Communication, 1*(1), 170–176.

Winston, C. (2023). *How to lose the hounds: Maroon geographies and a world beyond policing*. Durham, NC: Duke University Press.

Wolfe, R. N., & Johnson, S. D. (1995). Personality as a predictor of college performance. *Educational and Psychological Measurement, 55*(2), 177–185. https://doi.org/10.1177/0013164495055002002

Youth Justice Coalition. (2019, July 12). About the space. https://youthjustice la.org/about-the-space/

Zembrodt, I. (2021). Commitment: Predicting persistence for low-SES students. *Journal of College Student Retention: Research, Theory & Practice, 23*(3), 580–606. https://doi.org/10.1177/1521025119858340

Index

Founded in 1893,
UNIVERSITY OF CALIFORNIA PRESS
publishes bold, progressive books and journals
on topics in the arts, humanities, social sciences,
and natural sciences—with a focus on social
justice issues—that inspire thought and action
among readers worldwide.

The UC PRESS FOUNDATION
raises funds to uphold the press's vital role
as an independent, nonprofit publisher, and
receives philanthropic support from a wide
range of individuals and institutions—and from
committed readers like you. To learn more, visit
ucpress.edu/supportus.